2018-2019

To: Mrs. Haar

Thank you for being so
Supportive! I appreciate you.
Happy Holidays!
Love,
Daniela Kovatch

Captured Fireflies: Truths, Mistakes, And Other Gifts Of Being an English Teacher

Captured Fireflies

Truths, Mistakes, And Other Gifts Of Being an English Teacher

Meredith Newlin

Cover Design © 2017
by Jessica Perkins Moncla
Author Photograph
by Catherine Guerrero
Published by Realscolena Publishing
Durham, North Carolina
Second Edition
2018
ISBN:
9781979527071

ISBN-13: 1979527075

LCCN: 2017917567
BISAC: Language Arts & Disciplines / Study & Teaching

For Emily, and for all teachers who strive to create a new thing, a new attitude, a new hunger

And for Eleanor, Oscar, and Catherine - my world

Like Captured Fireflies

In her classroom our speculations ranged the world.
She aroused us to book waving discussions.
Every morning we came to her carrying new truths, new facts,
new ideas
Cupped and sheltered in our hands like captured fireflies.
When she went away a sadness came over us,
But the light did not go out.
She left her signature upon us
The literature of the teacher who writes on children's minds.
I've had many teachers who taught us soon forgotten things,
But only a few like her who created in me a new thing, a new
attitude, a new hunger.
I suppose that to a large extent I am the unsigned manuscript of
that teacher.
What deathless power lies in the hands of such a person.

—John Steinbeck (1955)

CONTENTS

Meredith Newlin

PREFACE

You know that dream where you're standing in front of a full class of students and you're wearing nothing but your underwear? In my fourth year of teaching, that dream nearly became a reality, although I'm not sure if that kind of mortifying dream would have been worse than what really happened.

It was a regular Tuesday in November, just three days before my thirty-second birthday. My afternoon class of twelfth graders was getting ready to start act 2 of *Macbeth*. They say if you say "Macbeth" three times, it's bad luck. Maybe that's why it happened.

It would take one student, Jacob, two minutes to say two sentences from the play, and his time was one of the fastest in the class. Jacob, who had pensive, deep brown eyes, was one of the kindest students I'd ever taught. He also had autism and loved playing the trumpet.

"Thank you for the lesson!" he would say at the end of each day. He had been in my freshman class my second year of teaching. It had been an honors class. Now, three years later, he was in my senior class. It was not an honors class.

4

It was a class where the dynamic was very— I'm rubbing my chin to try to find the precise word and will settle on— *interesting*. My principal had delicately told me during an observation early in the school year that I might be "walking a fine line." He had always been very supportive and appeared to see only the best in me. So it took me awhile to realize that he didn't really mean that phrase as a compliment. At the time, I thought he meant it was a skill that I had. After all, to walk a fine line would be like walking a tightrope, right? Which took talent, patience, and precision, didn't it? So wasn't walking a fine line a good thing? I neglected to realize that walking a tightrope increased one's chances of falling far and falling hard.

My principal had explained, "I mean, it's great that they feel so comfortable in your class. That's good! You seem to have a great relationship with them. But it seems like your control is just a little bit too . . . loose. You're just . . . walking a fine line." Then he added graciously, "I don't know. Maybe it'll work. You know the class better than I do. I just don't want you to have to stress out about it."

A couple of months later, I had come to tire of walking that fine line. The only thing that was like a tightrope was my patience. And on this November day, I'd had enough of this class. There was Danny, who had his ears pierced with circular black discs that widened his earlobes. He was always laughing and talking while I was talking. There was Courtney, a dancer who sat quietly in the front and tried to pretend like she wasn't there. There was Chris, who was cheerful and very sweet but easily distracted by Danny as well as Keaton, Carlos, Thomas, and Matthew, who always came in together. I taught at a magnet school, and the six football players had been bused in from Northern High School and wore matching khakis and white polo shirts, their school uniform. They carried themselves very slowly and deliberately. We usually had mutual respect.

Then there were Julia and Destiny, who came in late every single day. Destiny was always high. On this particular day, they came in ten minutes late. We'd already been working on our journals. I say "we" because I wrote with them. More on this momentarily.

When the girls came in late, they muttered something to Keaton, and the quiet journal writing was immediately disrupted. I sighed, then asked Julia, Keaton, and Destiny to work outside. My classroom was in a trailer, so that meant they would have to work outdoors.

Soon I heard the three of them again raising their voices and getting off task, and I knew I'd have to go out there to do some redirecting. I jotted down my last thoughts in my journal, left it on the lectern, then went outside to check on them. Three minutes later I was engrossed in a motivational speech to them about the importance of trying harder as they looked off into the distance with their eyes glazed over.

At this point, you may be making a mental checklist of all of the teaching mistakes this story has thus far illuminated. You would be absolutely correct in doing so, but I haven't even gotten to the most egregious mistake yet.

In the middle of my motivational speech, Julia suddenly interrupted, declaring that she needed to go inside to get her purse. She, of course, was just tired of listening to my lecture.

When she came back out, she glared at me. The malevolent look was nothing new from her, but she seemed especially put out.

Then Jacob came out very distraught, shaking his head and covering his ears. "I don't want to go back in there," he muttered.

"What is it, Jacob?" I asked, concerned that maybe someone had teased him.

"People are being mean. It's bad. I'm not going back in there."

Well, that was it. Nobody teased Jacob on my watch. Or even on my lack thereof. I asked Julia to get back to work, but she held her hand up in front of my face.

"No, you already done said I make you 'nuts,' so I don't want to hear anything else from *you*," she retorted. She made quotation marks with her fingers when she said the word "nuts."

What could she have been talking about?

I heard a loud noise just before I walked back in the room.

When I came back in, the class was silent. Some were just looking down. Nobody looked at me.

"Well, what is it?" I asked Courtney. She sat with Jacob closest to the front, a couple of feet from my desk.

Her mouth was open, and her face looked like she had just seen an iguana flying an airplane.

"Somebody just read your journal out loud!" she finally spat out.

My heart dropped to my toenails. And my face flushed, likely a nice shade of watermelon with a few tinges of eggplant.

"What?"

With my eyes about to jump out of their sockets, I turned to the class, looking simultaneously for any sign of either mutiny or loyalty from any of them, searching their faces for clues about who the perpetrator could be. Keaton? No, he had been outside. Danny? Maybe. Matthew? No, he was too shy and hung on every word I said. Chris? Possible, but doubtful.

Of course, this journal wouldn't be full of my everyday mundane thoughts, such as how much I hated folding laundry or a list of frozen food items I needed to purchase from the grocery store on my way home. This journal was full of my darkest secrets and details about intimate relationships. All of my self-doubt; all of my emotional problems; all of my messy, uncooked, slimy, stinky *feelings*. It would have been less embarrassing if I could have just wet my pants in front of all of them.

And to top it all off, on this current day's page I had written, "*I am so tired. I just want to go home. Julia and Destiny are late again, and they are now getting everyone distracted. They drive me nuts!*"

So all of those personal feelings and thoughts were now out there, flying around this classroom and forever changing the natural energy of the hour and a half that these young people and I would spend together.

I had myself to blame for leaving my journal in full view on the front lectern. But they were to blame, too.

I threw up my hands and said, "Well, this takes the cake. I give up. That you guys would do this is just incredible. I'm in shock. I'm flabbergasted. This is about as low as you could go. Congratulations."

My passive-aggressive guilt trip seemed to have no effect. Nobody laughed. Nobody moved. I didn't know what to do except call the school counselor, Mitzi.

I stepped outside with my body half in and half out the door so that the students wouldn't see my tears or hear my voice shaking. But, really, why did I care anymore? Mitzi got someone to cover my class, and I went to her office and bawled. When I was finished bawling, she called in Julia and Destiny and spoke to them in my defense, but they were even more disrespectful than ever. The assistant principal then called me in with Julia and Destiny. She said to the girls, "I know y'all are mad right now. But you're gonna have so many teachers throughout your whole life. You know some of 'em care, and you know some of 'em really don't. Now you got one who cares. And that's what it comes down to."

Whatever she said seemed to appease them.

Still, I took the next two days off, enjoyed my birthday, and didn't come back until I was thirty- three years old, which was the following week.

Upon my return, the awkwardness was palpable. I merely went through the motions with the class. I gave no sign of caring about them and offered no emotional availability whatsoever. I was basically just a warm body.

"Can I play Macduff in the last act?" Danny pleaded at the beginning of class. I just shrugged.

"Sure, whatever," I replied, not looking up.

Later that week, in the computer lab, I made my routine check of their research paper checklists. When it was Keaton's turn, he came up to my desk but didn't go away after I had put the requisite check in the box on his sheet showing that he'd completed his ten note cards. Instead, he slid his chair back and put his elbows on his knees, looking up at me. "So when you gonna come back?" he asked, almost accusingly.

"I *am* back," I replied, not understanding. "I've been back for three days."

"I mean *really* back," he responded. "When you gonna come back? When you gonna come back. . . and be our *teacher*." His big brown eyes widened, then twinkled just a bit. I sighed. And I couldn't help but crack a smile. That's when I realized it would have to stop being about me.

From that point on, something thawed in me. I decided to try to relax. When I stopped to notice, there were no longer any discipline issues with that class. There was quiet, calm respect. We worked together. Sometimes we even laughed with each other. When they finished their final exams, I let them play some of Tupac's music in my class, and they were surprised to learn I knew all the words to "California Love."

Our humanity was now common, at the same level. They now knew I didn't have all my stuff together. A day I never thought I'd ever recover from turned out to be some pretty good fertilizer.

Four years later, my birthday week was a bit less dramatic. One of my eighth graders asked, "Ms. Newlin, what you want for your birthday? Tell you what; I'm gonna double your salary."

I replied, "Oh, is that so? That sounds nice."

The student said, "Yep, my dad sells insurance. I'm gonna make it happen."

Later in the day, another student asked, "What you want for your birthday, Ms. Newlin?"

I replied, "Well, I just found out someone is going to double my salary for my birthday."

Her response: "Oh. Well, I can't do that." Then she appeared to realize something and said brightly, "But I could bring you a doughnut!"

She made me laugh, and then she laughed, too. That kind of moment, that simple little glimmer of light that ever so quietly radiates right smack in the middle of my heart, is what I consider one of the many captured fireflies of teaching. That's when I feel like a success.

Those moments can be a long time coming sometimes.

Take Jennifer Cooper, for example. She first entered my Advanced Placement (AP) English Language and Composition class in August 2005.

She hated me.

She came in late and sat in the back of the class. She glared, rolled her eyes, whispered, doodled, and always seemed to be snickering at—as all new, insecure teachers tend to perceive—me. She thought I was a flake, and I thought she was a brat.

I immediately set out to charm Jennifer. I tolerated her tardiness and her jokes. I complimented her writing and sometimes let her get away with certain behavior when I should have been tougher, like when I knew she was behind me making mocking gestures during a class discussion or when I could smell the cigarette smoke on her after she came back from lunch. She wore outlandish, nonsensical outfits, like a heavy parka in August or a miniskirt with no stockings in February. She was a couple heads shorter than me, and with her short, dark brown hair, she reminded me a little of Winona Ryder in the movie *Heathers*, and I told her so. I meant it as a compliment and a bonding offering, but my intentions didn't meet with an enthusiastic response.

So things went on like that. She mocked me; I ignored her. We had an understanding.

Yet somehow, before I knew it, Jennifer slowly started to grow on me. There was a tenderness and sensitivity that she slowly revealed, mainly through thoughtful responses during class discussions, or through quietly brilliant poems she would nonchalantly hand to me after the dismissal bell rang and the class trickled out. She bared her soul and emotions to me and, as I soon learned, to anyone who would listen. After I encouraged her to get in touch with an editor of a local poetry magazine who might be able to mentor her about getting her work published, I soon came to recognize my slow, subtle influence upon Jennifer. Even though some of the time she could be irrationally moody and frowned for no apparent reason, every now and then she would laugh at one of my dumb jokes before she could stop herself. It became easy to be her cheerleader.

One day I learned Jennifer would not be in class for a while. She was going to be sent away out of state for a couple of months for treatment for alcohol addiction. When she came back, it was her senior year, and we thought she had gotten better. She seemed to be back to her healthy, upbeat, cheerful self. She cared about her grades and wanted to stay on track.

Pretty soon after that, Jennifer received out-of-school suspension for possession of drugs on campus. Together, administration and teachers held meetings about her: "What are we going to do with Jennifer? We cannot have this—not on our campus." Of course, we all cared about her, and we all loved her. But "You know how cunning and wily she is; you know how she manipulates. We've all coddled her too much. We have to keep her on a tight leash. Let's just make certain she graduates." In other words, if we could just get her out of there, we could all breathe a sigh of relief.

In these meetings, I nodded my head vigorously and stayed fairly silent. I didn't stand up for Jennifer or come to her defense. I took part in the collective giving up on her. I allowed myself to lose sight of the cheerful, talented, spunky, loving Jennifer who had grown on me and trusted herself to me. I felt guilty about doing this. I knew deep down that she wasn't just another rebel without a cause who had succumbed to teenage angst.

I wanted Jennifer to know the truth: that focusing on her purpose could prove so much more interesting than getting drunk or high. Somewhere beneath her attention-starved façade was a dreamer with a goal, and she needed to hold on to that. So I did something I was probably not supposed to do. (It would not be the first time I did this as a teacher.) I wrote her a letter:

> *Dear Jennifer,*
>
> *I want you to know that I am writing a book. I started it a few months ago, but the day you asked me whether you would make a good English teacher has helped inspire me to really delve into it. I have already gotten 90 pages so far. It's going to be all about teaching, and I am indirectly writing it to you, because it's full of all the things I would want you to know if you ever do*

decide to become an English teacher—not that I am pressuring you to stick to that as your dead-set career choice, but I really do think you'd make a great one. So in a way, this book is going to be my gift to you.

In return I ask that you continue paying attention, contributing your meaningful insights, and sharing your poetry when you feel like it throughout these last seven weeks of Creative Writing class. In addition to being your naturally brilliant and wonderful self, it would also mean a lot if you would not goof off anymore at school. It really makes me worry. (When you become a teacher, you will understand that we already have way too much to worry about.)

There was a message in a fortune cookie I got one time—I'll pause here since I know you are laughing right now that I abruptly transitioned to a fortune cookie anecdote. Are you done? Okay.

There was a message in a fortune cookie I got one time—actually I think it was about five years ago— that read, "The best times of your life have not yet been lived." Jennifer, it was the best thing I have ever read in my life. I taped it to my mirror, and it has been there ever since. And it has proven to be undeniably true. Whenever I am having a tough day, week, or year, I remember that fortune cookie message.

No matter how pointless things may seem at the moment, every day really does turn out to be more beautiful and meaningful than the last. The more I get into life, the more I love it, and the more I can't wait to find out what comes next—even with the headaches, frustrations, and seemingly endless struggles. I think that you will find the same to be true as you grow along this journey of life. I believe there is a world of promise waiting for you after graduation, and I know you will tackle your challenges with courage and grace. I can't wait to hear about all of your adventures in the years to come.

So back to the whole point of this letter: basically, I am asking you for a favor. I am asking you

*to keep this letter as proof that I said I was going to
write a book. I am asking you to help hold me to it,
since I will know that you are counting on me. I am
writing this book for you. No matter how daunted and
frustrated I will undoubtedly get when I will have to
overcome the hurdles of the publishing logistics, getting
an agent, etc., I am hereby promising to you that I
WILL write this book, and when I do, I will dedicate
it to you. Even if you don't end up becoming an English
teacher. So I am counting on you to
hold me to my word. (No pressure!)*

*I am also counting on you to buy it when it gets
published. After all, I could use at least one gallon of
milk.*

Thank you.

With love,

Ms. Newlin

I never got to give Jennifer the letter, because she went away again and didn't return. She found an alternate way to graduate, but I never got to say good- bye.

Seven years passed. In those seven years, I taught in two more different schools and experienced even more of the highs and lows of teaching: everything from an entire cafeteria of eighth graders cheerfully singing "Happy Birthday" to me like one gigantic Von Trapp family, to a student who told me in front of the whole class to "just do your damn job, bitch." (Should I have capitalized the "b" in that last sentence? The conundrums we English teachers face!)

Anyway, on a sunny Sunday last July, I received a letter (well, a Facebook message, to be exact.) It was not from Jennifer, but from a different former student who, without knowing it, encouraged me to continue plugging away writing this book and not give up. Moments before, I had been lamenting the lack of momentum and the writer's block I was experiencing to get through finishing the draft of this book. The message I'd heard at church about faith and perseverance had helped me not at all. That afternoon I was at the pool wrangling my two small children when I quickly checked my phone and saw this:

> *Mrs. Newlin, I am not sure if you remember me well, or at all. You taught my ninth grade English class, several years ago. However, I wanted to share with you the impact that that short year had on my life. It was after high school that I realized I wanted to be a teacher. I wanted to help young people grow, and flourish, and explore their talents, as my teachers have helped me. John Steinbeck says, "I have come to believe that a great teacher is a great artist and that there are as few as there are any other great artists. It might even be the greatest of the arts since the medium is the human mind and spirit." I could not find a truer quote that embodied teaching. Yes, you taught me all about grammar, and synonyms, and the power of poetry, but you also taught me that a little bit of kindness can really go a long way. That teachers play such a powerful role, not only as a mentor but as a guide, as a beacon of wisdom and kindness.* A bright light of empathy for those of us that were always trapped in the dark. I want to sincerely thank you, for being that teacher for me and countless others. You were the one who inspired me to help the world the only way I know how, through teaching. Thank you so much for that.
> With love, Emily

This message knocked me off my feet—or it would have if I hadn't had to chase my one-year-old, who had just started learning how to walk. For a millisecond, I was able to see with crystal-clear vision what my teaching purpose really is.

You see, what is often going through my head as a teacher is something like this: "Here I go, late again yet another day. I need to get in more grammar and vocabulary this week. I need to be more technologically astute. I should post more on Twitter. But nobody ever "likes" my tweets. Maybe that stack of essays will grade itself. I really should be a tougher grader. Gosh, could my desk be any messier?

Where is the Lysol so I can disinfect some of this stuff? I really wish my fourth-block students had not written their Instagram handles for their first- block friends to see on my whiteboard right before the bell rang. They did it when I wasn't looking, thinking I wouldn't notice. Ah, they always get one past me. I should be stricter. I should do more blended learning. I should use more fun learning games with the Smart Board. Someday I will learn how to align it myself instead of always asking a student to get up and do it. I'm out of tissues again, and I still haven't gotten that pencil sharpener fixed. I haven't finished my Professional Development Plan. Because after thirteen-plus years, I still don't really understand how or why to do it. I really should crack down on tardies. I've had the same essential question on my whiteboard for the past week. Okay, the past two weeks. How can I grab and keep my students' attention today so that they'll learn as much as they can? Did I get through at all to that student in the hall yesterday? I hope my administrator thinks I am rigorous and dynamic and organized enough when she comes to observe me next week. Uh-oh, here come the kids down the hall about to enter my room. They look like they're about to walk into Folsom Prison. Oh, that's right; it's Monday morning and they don't yet drink coffee, and many of them don't eat breakfast, and they have a quiz today. That's why they hate me right now. At least that's what I'll tell myself. Deep breaths. This, too, shall pass. Smile."

These are the thoughts running through my head during any given teaching day. However, receiving Emily's message helped me realize that maybe sweating the small stuff, as they say, is really not all that important. Maybe it's okay to let go and put kindness first. Maybe that's why I'm here—not to be perfect, but to be kind. And maybe a little passionate as well.

What is the definition of successful teaching anyway? For some teachers, it is measured in test scores, documents, awards, and other accolades. For others, it is measured in how much their students have learned and grown, in the respect accorded them by colleagues or institutions, or maybe in their level of popularity with staff and students, or simply in the sense of meaning and purpose that fills a day and a classroom.

For me, successful teaching is any day when the shining joy of my profession seeps so deep into my bones that I am humbled by the gratitude and amazement I feel just to be alive. It's a day when quitting seems ludicrous because there is so much to be done, when I have set high expectations for myself and my students, and we have all embraced the challenge. When I think about it, I believe successful teaching happens when I

> build and grow a support network, smile, laugh,
> let my ego take a backseat, am
> willing to start all over, give my
> students choices, give my students
> structure, communicate clearly,
> listen with my whole being, am
> vigilant,
> learn from my mistakes,
> admit when I'm wrong (ugh! hate that one) let my
> passion outweigh my frustration,
> try to use new technology,
> have a healthy outlet for my emotions, accept
> imperfections (my own and others'),
> view parents as allies,
> take care of myself,
> delay immediate gratification, feed my
> passion for my subject,
> dare to engage and collaborate with
> colleagues,
> protect my learning environment, dare to
> expand my horizons,
> choose to not take things personally,
> establish and maintain mutual respect,

give it all to the Divine Chaos of the Universe,
and
err on the side of kindness.

There are two things most everyone can agree on about being a
teacher today in the United States: (1) public education is imperfect,
and (2) nobody has all the answers. If the opposite were the case, the
public educational system would be a utopia of rigor, excellence, and
success on all levels. Instead, we are experiencing the unprecedented.
Public education is getting a bad rap, and it seems everyone is
buying into the skewed narrative. Fewer and fewer college
graduates are choosing to become teachers, and many who *do*
become teachers don't stay in the profession for long. Education
in America has become a pendulum, apparently full of only the
lowest of lows and the highest of highs. Certain documentaries
paint a dire picture of low school morale, low expectations, low
graduation rates, and low test scores, while everything else is high:
high rates of teacher incompetence and shortages, high incidences
of school violence, high student-to-teacher class ratios—heck,
even the students themselves are high.

In my opinion, part of all this stems from disillusionment due
to a severe lack of information and guidance—I mean the real,
nitty-gritty, in-the- trenches information—available to new
teachers.

Instead what we usually get are thick, pedantic textbooks with
titles like "Infallible Instructional Delivery for the 21st Century,"
or "How to Be a Master of Classroom Management in Two
Days." With a few notable exceptions, most such books are
written in a detached, superior tone and include lots of tidy,
outdated pictures of perfectly posed students from precisely
diverse backgrounds, with their golf shirts neatly pressed and
buttoned, their hair eerily combed into flawless place, and their
faces forced into frozen smiles as they pore together over a
textbook that's always somehow opened to the exact middle page.

These misleading images imply that teachers must have their
work cut out for them. Apparently, students are nothing more
than well-dressed, nonresponsive mannequins sitting mutely and
passively at their desks, who will excitedly engage in whatever

assignment, procedure, or activity you ask them to do, as long as it comes from a suggested lesson plan from the standard course of study.

Despite the pretty pedagogical picture these books portray, a teacher and his or her classroom are not robotic, efficient, and flawless. A classroom is spontaneous, messy, jumbled, and imperfect. It can be full of beautiful surprises. Like in the hit animated movie *Inside Out*, it can be a chaotic control room of emotions, pulling you into joy, anger, elation, disgust, fear, embarrassment, and 15 bazillion other feelings. Just when you think joy is in control, all the different energies emanating from all those brains and hearts in your classroom can throw you a curveball if you are not careful. A classroom is not always streamlined, logical, and rational, even for those teachers who are always streamlined, logical, and rational. For the first year or two—or six, or thirty—teachers are honestly doing everything they can to survive. Veteran teachers who are positive, energetic, and organized and who have been thrice nominated "Teachers of the Year" have still been known to have classes they just can't reach, that make them cry at the end of the day. Sometimes even the best-planned lessons and efforts don't work with certain students, no matter how much time and preparation go into them.

But nobody, including English teachers, ever seems to want to let on how much they may be struggling. Nobody ever wants to admit that teaching can be really hard sometimes.

"Me, having a problem?" our demeanor and carriage convey to our colleagues and students. "Never!" We take ourselves seriously or cover up our problems to try to make everything seem effortless and seamless. At least that's what I did.

Maybe after a few years, it will actually be effortless and seamless for me. But for now, it's tough. I don't think it's fair for anyone to mislead you and say that it's not. I think the right thing to do is to be as real with you as I can get.

When I graduated from college, my parents and grandfather gave me a short little rite-of-passage book by Maria Shriver called *Ten Things I Wish I'd Known . . . Before I Went Out into the Real World*. (Think Dr. Seuss's *Oh, the Places You'll Go!* but longer, without as much rhyme, and with significantly more references to Shriver's then-husband, Arnold Schwarzenegger.) Although Shriver's book didn't necessarily *protect* me from things I would eventually have to learn for myself the hard way, she gave me a unique preview of them. She offered simple, down- to-earth advice about "adulting," as some call it today, that I, consciously or not, took to heart. Her book made a significant difference in my attitude toward and perception of all of those adult responsibilities and challenges that I eventually did encounter when I went out into the real world.

With all the various books on teaching methods, pedagogy, classroom management, and content knowledge, what exactly is the necessity of the one you're reading now? What qualifies me as the expert? Well, actually, I don't claim to be a teaching expert. But that's kind of the point. If anything, this book is a living, breathing, messy, tired, honest look at what teaching is really like in all its imperfect perfection. It is not my personal philosophy of education theory. It is not intended as a reference book for every English teacher. It is not a glorification of what a perfect and wonderful teacher I am because I am not. I'm quirky. I've never known how to quite fit in. I'm not a darling of my school system because I don't have the system figured out (but if you happen to think that not having the system figured out is actually more of a strength than a weakness, then maybe this book is for you.) Even my late Grandpa Kemp (who was unwaveringly convinced that all of his grandchildren could do no wrong) saw my flaws as a teacher within five seconds the first time he visited my classroom. He and my Gramma Gail cheerfully delivered doughnuts to my eleventh graders one sunny May afternoon after they took their AP English exam. Before they left, Grandpa whispered to me, "Don't forget. Be tough on 'em." (After he had just given them doughnuts.) Anyway, not to worry, I will get to all of my flaws throughout the book and hopefully elucidate why and how they can be useful at times.

I believe sharing our flaws and mistakes makes us stronger. This book is a response and a reflection, and, at times, what I hope will be helpful advice. But it's not necessarily my preachy advice to *you*; in fact, it is more my advice to *me*: my fresh, hopeful, new teaching self those first few weeks of school—the simple, logical, useful things I wish I had known, really *known*, and not just been warned into believing. It could have made it all a bit easier to understand and deal with if I would have had a simple, straight-shooting quick read, not a long reference book through which to pore.

Two of my favorite writers are Lee Smith and Elizabeth Gilbert. In one of the several talks by Smith that I have seen or attended, she explained how she long ago followed the advice of one of her Hollins College English professors to "write about what you know." And in Gilbert's book *Big Magic*, Gilbert asks, "Do you have the courage to bring forth the hidden treasures that are hidden within you?" Those calls to action are my anchors in writing this book. The place from which I am writing is to let someone know what I know—the thrill, the pain, the challenge, the rewards—everything I can possibly tell you (within the limits of word count, my job, and, I admit it, the blessing and approval of my parents and, someday, my children) about what it's like to be a teacher before you get into it (or, maybe, *after* you've already gotten into it and are asking yourself what you've gotten into!)

Another place from which I write comes from another favorite writer, Henri J. M. Nouwen, who kept a diary that he considered his "inner voice" of guidance during a time of great upheaval and confusion, which eventually became his simple yet meaningful book, *The Inner Voice of Love: A Journey through Anguish to Freedom*. This book represents my "inner voice" of reason and grounded pragmatism that emerges when I give myself time to think calmly and clearly, to reflect, revise, ruminate, and, above all, be gentle and loving with myself (something we teachers have been known to struggle with at times). This is the best that I have to give as a teacher. This book is a list of reminders, not just to you, but also to myself, of which I constantly strive (keyword: *strive*) to be vigilant.

And yet there is still another reason for this book. I have always wanted to write, and even when I didn't fully acknowledge it to myself, I have always wanted to teach. So it goes without saying that when I first started teaching, all I wanted to do was write about it. Because, after all, who wouldn't want to talk about falling in love? I fell head over heels in love with teaching, and I fell fast.

When I began teaching, I was overwhelmed. I needed to express what was happening and how important and vital the job made me feel. I would take nearly every opportunity or excuse to send out a hastily typed group email with the subject line "Teaching moment!" to any friend or family member who would read it. These emails were usually along the lines of "You won't believe what Susie Student did today!" or "My principal paid me a compliment!" or other insignificant occurrences that I thought meant everything at the time.

For some reason or other, my friends and family actually put up with this and read those trivialities. "Look at me, friends and family!" is what I was really saying in those emails. "I am a *teacher*." Other times my emails would be a little too soul- revealing. "You need to put that back inside your brain and not let it out again," an acquaintance admonished after I sent a sixteen-hundred-plus-word email about a stressful saga involving a missing testing manual. "That was what we call *too much information*."

But I really did want to sound my barbaric yawp over the rooftops of the world. There was something so artful, dramatic, and honorable about the job that even I had to admit. I relished any and all gushing. For example, I loved hearing, "Oh, *wow*. You're so *brave*. I don't know how you *do* it!" anytime I uttered those proud words, "I am an English teacher," to new friends, to new neighbors, to old classmates, even to the occasional convenience store clerk. What I was doing in my job was filled with drama: conflict, heroism, cowardice, beauty, repulsion, anger, euphoria—all the makings of a reality show on Bravo!

Teaching is one long emotional roller coaster, and I wrote this book as a way to hang on. I wrote it because of the way teaching makes me feel inside. I wrote it as a way to celebrate the times that went inexplicably well and as a way to stay sane during the times that went inexplicably wrong. (Don't worry, I'll get to most of them later.) Part of this book comes from simple notes of embarrassing admissions if only to myself, when I just didn't know what to do after an especially difficult or stagnant class, or when I didn't even know that what I had been doing was all wrong.

There are so many things I wish I had known at that time about all the elephants in the (class)room, like how students really act and react; what they really do, say, and think; what influences they encounter and are under. One peek at some of their journals or notes will give you a preview. Forget merely skipping class, smoking cigarettes, or experimenting with alcohol or sex. These days students are cutting themselves; attacking their teachers and recording it on YouTube, Instagram, or Facebook Live; battling anorexia and bulimia; or popping Dad's prescription Xanax for a lunchtime buzz—and these are the so-called good kids, raised in loving, privileged homes.

I wish I had known how all of these factors come into play when we teachers are supposed to be filling our instructional duties so dutifully. I wish I had known how in a matter of seconds the classroom can become a quiet cauldron, and you are the only person in the room who doesn't understand why.

You won't find out how to deal with that in your teacher's manual or job description. I wish I had known all of the things that happen in teaching that are too ugly and embarrassing and non-politically correct to discuss. We continue to ignore or not discuss what is really happening, and then we wonder why things are not getting better and teachers don't stay in the profession. It is only through the doing of it that I have learned how to survive as a teacher, not through some detached manual handed out to the masses as they exit the mandatory "New Teacher Orientation" week.

What makes it all happen? How does it all come together? What makes it work, and what makes it fail? In theory upon educational theory, do any of them provide the one authoritative, magical answer?

A number of books about teaching that I have borrowed, bought, or been given have proven invaluable. So if you do want some recommendations for helpful books about teaching and/or teaching English, I have listed some of those here and mentioned others throughout the book. In humble, well-organized profound, wise language, they offer potent classroom management medicine and creative lesson plan ideas, and many teachers, myself included, would be lost without their guiding voices. They include Jim Burke's *The English Teacher's Companion* (2013); *Teaching Outside the Box* (2016), by LouAnne Johnson; *The Courage to Teach* (2017), by Parker J. Palmer, and *What Great Teachers Do Differently* (2012) by Todd Whitaker.

But even with their sage advice and insight, many of the authors of these wonderful books narrate their story from more near the *end* of their race. They have spent years training and figuring it all out. They have had years to earn the respect they are due. Whether they want it or not, they are the best of the best. Those of us who are walking into the classroom brand-new don't have those years of experience, and sometimes we don't always have the best training. At this point, we need some basic fuel to keep up our stamina. Teachers make at least a hundred little and big decisions a day, and those decisions can sometimes feel like the multiple choice tests we teachers inevitably have to administer: option A can seem right at the time, but it's only after you get backthat big fat "F" that you realize you should have chosen option B.

Another inspiring book I encountered was *Teacher Man* by Frank McCourt. Strangely enough, it was while I was googling *Angela's Ashes*, which I was once considering teaching to my AP seniors. I immediately went to Borders bookstore and could not find it under the Biography section or even Irish History, where it was listed as being shelved. I finally found it under Recommended Memoirs, right smack at the front of the store with the rest of the best sellers. I started reading it in the car (before I drove out of the parking lot of Borders, of course), went to sleep reading it, then woke up the next morning and continued reading it while making coffee and scrambling eggs. (This was in my pre-vegan days. If you happen to care about things like that.) Anyway, I fell in love with this book. Frank McCourt had taken nearly every teaching experience and emotion I had ever had and managed to put it on the page. His memoir was not only engrossing and entertaining; it was also informative, comforting, and motivating. In *Teacher Man* McCourt had taken what I was feeling and validated, acknowledged, and shared it.The part he wrote about hiding behind the teacher's desk to avoid facing an intimidating class as they enter? Check. The part about classroom chemistry and how you either have it or don't? Exactamundo. The part about not wanting to fill out forms or answer to bureaucratic crap? That was me completely. I read his entertaining "excuse note" lesson idea and stole it the very next week. I read his explanation that students asking about their teachers' personal lives was just their ploy to get off topic from the lesson, and I couldn't believe how utterly fooled I had been. (All this time I had really, truly thought that my students had actually *cared* about my life and *wanted* to hear my poems and funny stories about running marathons, quirky cats, kale, missed trains, and other mishaps in the south of Italy.)

A friend and writer, Sarah Kaplan Jones, volunteered her time to come as a guest speaker to my creative writing class. Her advice to my students was to pay attention to critiques but not to criticism. In this book nitpickers and naysayers may pounce on their share of both: "You didn't explain it like that; you didn't remember to mention this." Of course I didn't. Because I am not you.

I hope you will allow the following disclaimer: I am an English teacher but not a grammar fanatic. I reserve the right to use rhetorical questions, contractions, and end sentences with prepositions. Also, this is not intended as a sneering exposé of public education. In fact, in my opinion, the public school system is not nearly as hopeless or doomed as some people make it out to be. In fact, in many places, in many school systems, I daresay it might just be on the cusp of a rebirth. This also is not a "coulda, shoulda, woulda" book or simply a list of "dos and don'ts." And it certainly is not a book about pedagogy, since I don't have the authoritative qualifications to write one. I am an authority on what is great about being an English teacher and why you should be one if that's what you want to do. I am not rebellious, defiant, or jaded. I don't want to get fired. I don't really think it's necessary to rock the boat or buck the system in a self-destructive way in order to be a meaningful and effective teacher, and I hope this book helps to show you how. If you're a skeptic, a critic, or a "Yeah, but…" kind of person, then please do us both a favor and stop reading now and go seek some other flawless, expertly written handbook of perfection because these aren't the droids you are looking for. No, I'm just kidding.

Seriously, my hat's off to you. The world needs you. How else would any of us have the idea to label all the containers in our refrigerators? Your detail- oriented, rule-following ways serve many uses. But you and I are not alike because I'm an optimist, a Romantic, and a "Yeah, so what?" kind of person. And I still hope you find something useful to you in this book.

There has been no one person, no one mentor, and no one book that has helped me along the way in my first years of teaching. It was a bunch of different people, ideas, and experiences, sometimes all at once. Even others' mistakes and unconscious exemplars of how *not* to do things have helped me. Most of all, it was the stumbling and at times very embarrassing mistakes I proudly claim as my own, as well as the joy of learning that I am proud to have evoked in my students and in myself.

In his poetic essay "A Former Teacher," John Steinbeck wrote of the truths and insights he and his fellow students brought to his teacher, like captured fireflies. The title of my book is a representation of that truthful, inspiring teacher I and most of us strive to be, but also the title is indeed the book: these chapters are all my captured fireflies—a compilation of truths and insights my students have brought me every morning and afternoon without even knowing it, through their energy, vulnerability, courage, kindness, honesty, brilliance, and contagious laughter. As I repeatedly tell my students, they light up my life. They are the fireflies we teachers always must ultimately set free in order for them to shine their brightest.

The final reason I wanted to write this book was that I enjoy helping people. I try to be real.Making someone feel comforted, encouraged, and empowered is a thrill for me. And for some strange reason, some people sometimes listen to me and take my advice, and it seems to help them some of the time. I don't know you—not yet, at least—but the chance that you might be one of those teachers who could use some help, humor, and encouragement. is why I am writing this book.

Things I have come to know as a teacher are things I wish I had been directly taught but realize now that I have been taught all along. I had the best English teachers in high school, the best English professors in college, and experienced, extraordinary mentors when I began teaching, who guided me through every step. I have done the reading and listened to the lectures and attended the seminars, both the ones that were required and the ones I went to simply because I wanted to.

However, all of the books, lectures, and advice money can buy could never have truly prepared me for what I learned hands-on as a teacher. Nobody really ever can. Nothing—no guide, manual, or book, including this one—will truly prepare you for the mountaintops and valleys you will encounter in this profession. This book is what they didn't tell me, and what I am hoping to tell you. And if it helps you in any way along your journey, then writing it has been worth it.

HOW I GOT HERE IN THE FIRST PLACE

New English teachers run the gamut. Some walk into the classroom completely oblivious, with manuals from the state, and with good intentions and no clues. They're just trying to survive. Others are beyond prepared. (Maybe you are one of these people.) After a precise four years in a prestigious university, where they undoubtedly had a full teaching scholarship, never earned below a 3.94 GPA, and were expertly mentored into becoming master educators, they can hardly wait to implement everything they learned. They studied and fretted over the Praxis test, endured student teaching, and are now armed with feedback, observation notes, unit plans, lesson plans, classroom management skills, a general understanding of their teaching strengths and "areas for growth," and everything else necessary for absolute success and the utmost control in their new classroom. They walk into their first classroom, new teaching license in hand, and they know everything. And they know that their students will love that they know everything. They are prepared. They know precisely what is coming. They are more than ready.

I was not one of those teachers.

Surprisingly, I used to think I would be one of them, because, as it does for many prospective English teachers, the path appeared so simple, at least at first.

I grew up with a genuine, although not necessarily insatiable, passion for reading and writing. I mean, I definitely have never been a genius or anything, and maybe I loved reading and writing so much because it was of the few areas in which I excelled. My parents supplied my sister and me with plenty of opportunities to explore any sport or extracurricular interest, and except for Girl Scouts, I met most all of them with failed attempts. My participation in soccer and T-ball games consisted mostly of daisy-picking out in center field, highlighted by the occasional inept pass down the field (in the wrong direction) during the few times I actually did get the ball. When that happened, I felt victorious joy immediately followed by panicked terror; my teammates looked at me as if I were holding a ticking bomb that needed to leave my care as soon as possible. "Pass it!" they exclaimed in urgent exasperation. Their eyes seemed to plead, "Put that thing down before somebody gets hurt!"

Trying out for the swim team was an exercise in aquatic trauma. The flute was a dabbling interest. Under the careful tutelage of Mrs. Burris, piano looked temporarily promising until on the day of the recital I forgot the song I had memorized and sat there, frozen, until Mrs. Burris freed me from my misery and let me sit back down in the audience of the other three students and six parents in attendance. And after years of what might have turned into fervent dedication, even ballet and drama were surrendered.

It was pretty much the same with academics.

History was bearable, and science was decent, but after third grade, math was pretty much lost on me. Miss Ripley's elucidation of the multiplication tables and Ms. Barrier's nurturing patience in guiding me through pre-algebra were the last times I remember understanding and enjoying working with numbers.

What I never managed to fail at, however, were reading and writing. Ever since gentle, lovely Mrs. MacKay introduced us to "The Berenstain Bears" in kindergarten, I acquired an immediate and persistent love for books, and my mom encouraged reading, possibly thinking I might become a literary genius if she placed enough paperbacks of the classics in my Christmas stocking. She regularly compared me to Brigitta von Trapp (the brunette bookworm) from *The Sound of Music*. I shared this love for reading and writing with my classmate Anne Beatty (who has since become an accomplished English teacher and writer herself). I envied her dedication and attention span. She consistently won the "Book It!" contest every grading period, which meant she got a coupon for free pizza and her name displayed with a lot of stars next to it on Miss Ripley's big white reading incentive poster.

Anne and I had serious aspirations to cowrite a novel called "Come Out, Cat!" with what we considered at the time to be a compelling and highly original plot concerning, as the title hints at, a distraught nine-year-old in search of her beloved feline companion. We never got past a few dozen scribbled pages on a legal pad, but the hunger was there. I loved new spiral notebooks. New journals, new stories, new ideas for a book. I was a constant beginner.

English was the one area where I could never seem to fail. Whether they called it "language arts" in elementary school and middle school, "English" in high school, or "literature" in college, somewhere along the line, I saw that woman or man doing their thing up at the lectern, eruditely explicating a novel so vividly, passionately, and convincingly that something inside of me said, "That's it. That's for me. I can do that. *I want to be a teacher.*"

I was usually pretty much a dream student for almost every English teacher I ever had. I was never particularly brainy in other academic subjects, but when it came to reading and writing, I could knock it out of the park. This feeling that I could and should teach English became especially appealing when my sixth grade teacher, Miss McGill, who loved the Righteous Brothers, neatness and punctuality, and deep laughter, cleared her throat, held a paper in   front of her, and recited what I recognized as *my* essay to the class as a model, or when my high school English teacher, Mrs. Patty, gave us fun projects like reading biographies and giving presentations while dressed up as the famous person we'd read about. (I got really into my Katharine Hepburn costume.) Nothing much beat that rare, hard-earned "Excellent!" Mrs. Patty wrote at the top of my essays. As a pensive, reclusive introvert, this affirmation felt nice. Somebody believed in me and brought out my gifts. I wanted the power to make somebody else feel that way. Also, I'd always secretly enjoyed being a bit bossy. So I sought opportunities to work with kids who I could be in charge of, whether it was through babysitting, Girl Scouts, or volunteering to teach First Day School at my family's Quaker meeting. My parents had come from a long line of educators on both sides of their families and instilled in my sister and me a simple but unquestioned reverence for education; they brought us up to believe teaching was a worthwhile profession. My senior year of high school, I applied to be a North Carolina Teaching Fellow, which would have given me a full ride to college, but I didn't make the final cut. I still blame it on the fact that I spilled coffee all over the front of my dress on the way to the interview, which probably didn't make the best impression on the interview team.

But back to writing: the best part about it was that it came relatively easily. After all, they're just words. Words belong to almost all of us. Most all of us have access to them. Writing is not like sports or most of the arts. Beyond pencil and paper or a keyboard, writing doesn't require complicated gear, tools, instruments, or supplies. With words, we all have the same tools, the same clay. The way we choose words and arrange them on a page is completely up to us. And when people feel affected or moved or changed or amused by the way we choose and arrange our words, it feels good.

So after graduation, I signed up for the requisite English and education courses at the University of North Carolina at Asheville, and all signs were "go" for what I assumed would be an easy, uncomplicated ride on the "English teacher track." However, in the spring of my junior year, I learned that studying abroad in Paris would give me extra credits that would make a major in French easier than a major in English education. Choosing French would also make graduation in under four years more feasible. On top of that, in the spring before graduation, I heard of an internship at a travel magazine publisher in my hometown, which sounded like too promising an opportunity to pass up.

So I settled for a minor in English, picked up the major in French, and made an all-too-easy transition from college graduation to the grueling excitement of the working world. Then when the summer was over, the magazine position turned into a foot-in-the-door position as an administrative assistant (basically code word for "receptionist and Diet Pepsi runner"), which my family encouraged me to humble myself to accept, saying that when I wasn't answering phones, I would likely get to wear many other hats. My family turned out to be right. The administrative assistant position quickly turned into a fact-checker position, which turned into a proofreader/copyeditor position, which turned into a contributing writer position (with my name on the masthead! Woohoo!), which finally, one glorious day nearly two years later, turned into an official position as editorial assistant, and I knew I had *really* arrived. Before I knew it, I couldn't remember anything about ever wanting to be a . . . what was that? Oh, yeah, an English teacher.

That was the way it was for my first four years out of college. While former college classmates complained of a "quarter-life crisis" and jumped from job to job, I relished with pride (which always goeth before something, as they say) that I was slowly becoming *someone*. I had gotten over one heartbreak only to endure another one, and sought refuge in a highly social, distracted, scattered, exciting single-girl life and perceived my position as nothing other than an important, invaluable, promising— albeit deadline-impaired—young journalist (who had never earned a journalism degree) and editor for an award-winning, nationally renowned publishing company (that routinely carried out both mass and individual layoffs without warning).

I did everything I was asked and did it with a smile. I got raises without requesting them and assumed it would always be that way. I got almost all "excellent"'s on annual reviews and was told I had a "bright future" at the company. So what if I had an occasional tendency to miss the due date by a hair? So what if I couldn't explain the difference between Quark and Adobe

Acrobat Reader? So what if I messed up the fonts on a few important pages? (Inconsequential fonts at that, in my opinion; I didn't understand why I had to be bothered with such trivial details.) I had "talent." I was accommodating, caring, and easy to be around. I said, "Thank you," "Yes," and "Sorry." And I said them quite frequently.

However, there came a time when that was no longer good enough. I started hating working in a cubicle. I lost interest in the articles I was writing and, to kill the time, instead crafted lengthy emails to friends about trips, pets, and generic life thoughts.

My supervisors called me in to talk about how if I didn't start caring more about the fonts, my job would be on the line. I never really believed them.

To satisfy this hunger for something more, on my lunch hour I started volunteering with the Big Brothers Big Sisters program. The "little brother" I was assigned, Nathan, didn't seem to connect with me. I would go visit him at Erwin Elementary School, where I had been a student, and he never had much to say in response to my questions. So I chatted with the teacher about how I had taken education classes and had always thought I would be a teacher and slightly regretted not having followed through on that dream. Since Nathan wouldn't talk to me, I turned to the other students, who wouldn't *stop* talking to me.

One afternoon Nathan's teacher, Mrs. Carmichael, asked me if I would like to read a book to the class. Her room was lit only with lamps and was a very comfortable and nurturing environment. It was the same room where I had read books with Anne Beatty in our beloved Miss Ripley's class. My Erwin had been an "open" school, which, in a nutshell, meant student-centered, and it was now a Montessori school. Erwin was a safe utopia of creativity and love. Erwin gave students the freedom to be themselves.

***

Miss Ripley had been one of the reasons I wanted to be a teacher. When I arrived in third grade, Miss Ripley was the prettiest lady I'd ever seen besides my mom. She looked like a Revlon model. She always dressed comfortably in baggy pants and

Reebok sneakers. She had a question for my parents at the first parent-teacher conference of the year: "Why in the heck doesn't Meredith go with the others to the AG (Academically Gifted) class on Wednesdays?" As my mom tells it, she and my dad looked at each other and said, "Well, we wanted her to be in AG, but her second-grade teacher told us she wasn't 'AG material.'" But Miss Ripley thought differently. I soon found myself in the AG Class on Wednesdays having fun solving complex and challenging intellectual tasks with a lovably zany Mrs. Rubenzer, who taught us the meaning behind the idiom "Put your nose to the grindstone!" which we did with enthusiasm.

But third grade was the magic year. Miss Ripley taught us early about financial management by having us write mock job applications and mock checks to pay mock bills. She had us writing all the time, especially in spiral notebooks that served as journals. We could tell her anything, and she would write back. I beamed when I read in her neat handwriting: "Meredith, friendships sure can be tricky, can't they? You're one of my favorite writers! Keep up the great work!" She also made us write composition upon dreaded composition on various topics, always in cursive. I remember once being the only one who had to write one titled, "What Happens When a Student Doesn't Listen and Has to Write a Composition as a Consequence." She wrote math problems in which we starred in the problems: "Jay and Kevin have ten books and give two to Anne, then four to Chris. How many books are left?" Then she had us contribute our own written math problems and would use them for class assignments.

The class was comprised of students of several different ethnicities; she guided us all toward harmonious camaraderie with one another. We were all pals. For our class performance for the school to present what we'd been learning that year, we donned black sunglasses and lip-synced to Huey Lewis's' "Hip to Be Square." She came to our ballet performances and soccer games and music performances. She laughed with us. She made learning fun. But these things didn't mean she was our best friend. If we misbehaved, there were consequences. Nobody wanted the dreaded "check" next to their name—not because it would mean that anything necessarily tangible would be taken away from us; we just didn't want to experience her disappointment. However, Miss Ripley wasn't ruthless. One afternoon, I missed the school bus because I'd snuck out in the hallway to meet a friend from another class. Miss Ripley didn't reprimand or shame me; she just called my parents, then calmly explained how I'd missed the bus and that she'd be driving me home.

As third grade came to an end, my family was leaving for vacation a day before the last day of school. Miss Ripley was going to be getting married and moving to Atlanta. She had invited us all to her wedding. She had also given each one of us a graduation diploma that she had laminated. Mine read, "Presented to Meredith, for being not only beautiful but SMART!" (I still keep it in a frame behind my desk in my own classroom.) At that time in my life, few people called me beautiful or smart.
But she was a person in authority who saw me that way; in fact, she saw in all of her students nothing but potential and possibility. Now on that last day of third grade, I hugged good-bye to Miss Ripley. She held me in an embrace and snuggled her cheek next to mine for a full five minutes. Most of the other third graders just sat there and observed us quietly, as if this were perfectly normal. Then one of them finally asked, "How long are you two going to hug?"

Miss Ripley replied matter-of-factly, "We are not hugging. We are snuggling."

On our family's way to Ocean Isle Beach that afternoon, I remember lying down in the backseat of my parents' station wagon and starting to cry softly, tears of both joy and sadness. I was the happiest any nine-year-old could be. It was the end of a glory year. I'd been watered, given sunlight, and nurtured by the most wonderful, challenging, creative, lovely teacher I had ever had. Twenty-four years later, she came to my wedding and danced with me.

She is the teacher I aspire to be every day.

***

Mrs. Carmichael reminded me a little of Miss Ripley. She wrote messages to her students on big chart paper about what they were going to do that day, and she signed them, "Love, Mrs. C." We all sat in a circle, and I opened to where the class had left off—chapter 4 of Scott O'Dell's *Island of the Blue Dolphins*. After I read a few sentences, then paused to show the pictures to the class, a feeling of warmth and meaning suddenly flooded over me. The fourth graders seemed to drink up this delicious story, and their innocent, eager, spellbound eyes made me feel like we were exploring a whole new planet together. After reading the book to Nathan's class, I went home and googled "how to become a teacher."

When I went back to work the next day, a beautiful June Thursday, something completely shocking, humiliating, sad, horrible, wonderful, and liberating happened: I lost my distinguished, promising, important job. Yeah, we're not really supposed to admit if losing a job has ever happened to us in life, are we? And if we do, it's in confidential whispers and convenient euphemisms like "downsized." We may say we got "laid off," but everyone knows it just means we got voted off the island. And admitting we lost a job means we must bear some giant red flag of incompetence or redundant unnecessity; it's something to conceal, gloss over, move past, forget, ignore, deny, bury.

The layoff came out of nowhere after I came back from lunch, around 2:00 PM. I was working in my cubicle, finishing a short article about Eucommia trees (don't ask) when "Meredith, I need to see you in the conference room" came the stern command from our department's editorial director, whom I'll call Barbara.

Barbara was an unmarried, childless fifty- something workaholic who ate an organic granola bar every morning at 10:15 sharp. She had an endless pantsuit wardrobe and a shiny blonde utilitarian bob. She marched wherever she went but somehow made it endearing. I worshipped her. She built me up and praised every little thing I did right. She was an energetic, enthusiastic, encouraging, and, every so often moody, strong leader. She had just been promoted to a well-deserved position as vice president at the publishing company.

When I heard her call my name, at first I thought, *Well, they've already talked to me about the fonts. So this is it. They're finally going to reprimand me for emailing too much.* However, when I followed Barbara into the conference room, there was obviously something more serious going on. The head of human resources, whom I will call Maria, was already seated with an ominous white folder in front of her. I sat down and could feel my face turning red, but I remained silent as the words "The department is being completely reorganized, and your position is being eliminated" floated out of Maria's mouth.

Oh, was that so? Okay.

Shock and a bit of grief would come in a second, but do you want to know what my immediate instinctive reaction was?

Island of the Mother-Lovin' Blue Dolphins.

As with the protagonist in Kate Chopin's "Story of an Hour," my first, teensy, whispering emotion for the smallest fraction of a moment—just a nanosecond—was an intense, elated sense of *freedom*! It was the strangest sensation of something dying but being born at the very same time. I had no idea what was being born, but I knew it was happening, somewhere deep inside, right at that moment. (And this was not related to any possibility of my being pregnant.) I knew that things would be not just okay but even better than before. I knew that something beyond my wildest imaginings was waiting for me after all this.

But first would come the surreality of it all as I listened vaguely to instructions about forms to sign, an exit interview, turning in keys, promises not to sue the company, and what was included in the "severance package," which I found to be such an unusual term. "Severance" connotes "terminate," "eliminate," "reject." Then you have the word "package" juxtaposed right there next to it. (As an English teacher, I really appreciate the word "juxtaposed.") A package is something one usually perceives as exciting to receive in the mail, or a gift to unwrap, or a bundle of perks on an exotic tropical vacation. Weird.

At some point during all of this, Maria paused and asked if I had any questions. All I could do was continue to keep my eyes up and glazed open, which is what I do when I want to keep from crying. I'm always afraid if I look down, the tears will fall. When I didn't say anything in response, except for "I guess nothing really surprises me anymore," Barbara continued.

"I want you to know," she explained carefully, in a voice almost as low as a whisper, "as I have told you many times, that I think you are a very *nice* person, and you're a very talented . . . *writer.*" Her tone fell a little awkwardly down on the word "writer," as if she were embarrassed for me. "And I want you to pursue your writing, and go after that. Because I think that's your true passion."

Then she mentioned something about some of the company's magazines not bringing in the business like they used to and how I was a great person and that she would write me a recommendation letter, which seemed comforting and not quite as humiliating.

However, as she and Maria continued talking, I grew numb and then number. I began feeling a little like Will Ferrell in the comedy film *Old School* when he is shot with the tranquilizer gun. Barbara's and Maria's voices seemed to get deeper and slower, but I didn't have a nice, cool swimming pool in which to fall. So after the severance speech, I responded ingeniously with: "I guess I'm just kind of shocked right now. I guess I just kind of want to go home and be with my mom and dad if that's okay." Nothing in me wanted to fight this or sue the company or cause a ruckus. I only wanted to retreat and lick my wounds.

After we left the room, Barbara brought a box for me to pack my few things. I wasn't shedding a single tear but shaking as I gathered my various cubicle accoutrements—an Eiffel tower lamp, framed family pictures, a stapler I contemplated pilfering but decided better not to— as quickly as possible. All I could think about was what a failure I felt like! And how ashamed I would be when I had to tell my friends and family! And what a loser I would seem like when I had to tell people! And what people would think when they found out!

Then I thought, *Oh, grow up.*

And I did. Somewhat.

Approximately one summer later, after a year of going back to a local university to pick up a few more necessary credits to earn an initial professional teaching license while scrambling to pay my mortgage by working as a substitute teacher, restaurant hostess, youth leader, camp counselor, tutor, freelance writer, house sitter, pet sitter, and even museum docent, I walked into another office: the office of an upbeat, energetic, forty-something principal at what would soon become one of *Newsweek*'s "America's Top 100 High Schools."

I'd just happened to show up at a teaching fair at a relatively new magnet arts/career technical high school called Weaver Academy that day. I had gone up to a friendly-looking tall man who was holding a clipboard and asked, "Um, excuse me. Are these the only schools with openings? Are there any more?" He replied, "Ah, actually, yes. An opening just came up at this very school. They're actually holding open interviews right now." A few minutes later, I was chatting with the principal about our shared Quaker roots and who my favorite teachers in high school had been. I mentioned Mrs. Patty. Turned out Mrs. Patty was working at that very school. In my interview with that principal, she told me to not say "sorry" anymore. The following week, she called me in for another interview. This time it was to sign a teaching contract, and Mrs. Patty was in the room, smiling. That principal knew I wasn't perfect, but she still put faith in my passion. With dozens of candidates from which to choose, she placed her bets on me and made a decision to believe in me. I'm so thankful she did. Little did I know just how lucky I was. I was going to be teaching at a school where all of the students wanted to be there. Many of them auditioned and applied to get in.

Thirteen years later, my everyday working world is no longer very glamorous and exciting: I am a schoolmarm with an ID lanyard (that I really should but usually don't wear), a monogrammed canvas tote bag, and a dime-store necklace given to me by a student that says "World's Best Teacher." My world is full of papers to grade, lessons to plan, adolescent angst, and the imposing standards of the state's End-of-Course testing, accountability, and curriculum guides.

And I love every minute it.

One other thing: when I had first started with that publishing company, the president's mother, an eccentric, lovable, seventy-something Southern belle with awesomely big hair, had come into the office one afternoon. I was asked to escort her to someone's office on another level of the building (and probably deliver somebody a Diet Pepsi as well, while I was at it). She always seemed sincerely interested in all types of people. Before we parted, she shook my hand but didn't let go. It sort of freaked me out for a second, but then she explained.

"See there, you've got a good handshake. . . .. I can feel your heart in your handshake," she said.
"And a great smile," she continued. "You've got what it takes."

I remember thinking that was one of the best compliments a person could ever receive. I decided to take that one with me, and I think I will pass it along to you: *You've got what it takes.*

THE NIGHTMARE AND THE DREAM SEAT

On some teaching days, it seems you are in total control. You're on a high and absorbing newfound energy from all these chatty, expressive, backpack- lugging fourteen-to-eighteen-year-olds. On any given day, they can be talkative, sullen, ingenious, infuriating, or dizzyingly ambitious. They defy all classification. Many days they crack you up and laugh at all of your dumb jokes (then other days, absolutely none of them). Some don't get you at all, while others might ostensibly put themselves in front of a bus for you. They are passionate, innocent, thoughtful, and loving. And you feel guilty and nervous about being that simultaneously irrelevant and influential because you are scared of the truth, which is that sometimes you don't have it all together, and sometimes you simply have nothing left to give.

Then the good days come back again and you remember why you wanted to be a teacher. And just when you think you finally do know what you're doing, you look at all the other experienced, wise teachers, and Awe, followed by her evil stepsister, Envy, creeps in. You long to have those wonder- teachers' apparent confidence, wisdom, energy, efficiency, and control. Even though those rock-star teachers can be indispensable mentors, you still sometimes feel like everybody thinks it's a competition of who attends the most football games, or who has the most master keys to all the different parts of the school—both literally and figuratively.

Your way of doing things is not always everyone else's way of doing things, and you learn the hard way that you *have* to do things their way sometimes. They're up there doing advanced ski jumps while you're still down there snowplowing it on the bunny slope. You are just there to teach, but you have to answer to so many people. You have to humble yourself. There are so many fires to put out. There are so many meetings, duties, plans, legalities, copies to make, papers to grade, parents to call, forms to complete, tasks, checklists, emails, details, documentations, and requests. You have to word everything just the right way. You have to be politically correct and stay objective. You must at least try to be up on technology. You have to assure everyone that you don't take things too seriously and, yes, you know that it's "just a job," when, for you, nothing is further from the truth.

You have to learn how to convey passion without being cheesy. You have to show your students how to read and write well and choose from myriad methods the best way to do that. You have to come up with insightful, thought-provoking questions to help them discover the beauty of words and stories. They need and deserve constant and varied outlets for their brilliance and creativity. Sometimes they test you and peg you as a naive pushover, but they just don't know how much time and effort you've put into your lessons. You can't directly tell them that, though, because—with all due respect, New Teacher—they simply don't care.

You have to spend a lot of time investigating, reviewing, and analyzing in order to know precisely what you are talking about. Sometimes you forget that you should never use a colon to separate a preposition from its object when you honestly detest the fact that you're supposed to care. You have to challenge your students, discipline them without having them perpetually resent you, push them to do better, use adequate "wait time," keep "high time on task," and come up with learning-driven lesson plans and focused, meaningful "essential questions." (It used to be you thought those were all bureaucratic buzzwords that are not really helpful or necessary, but you now realize that sometimes they really are.)

You desperately want to find new ways for your students to experience being an integral part of a wider community and world and to show them the importance of contributing their voices to that world. Sometimes they are already doing that, and you just sit back and watch them fly, although you can't help feeling a little left out, and even a little unnecessary. Sometimes you have great creative visions that don't come to fruition, and in the end, your best intentions weren't worth anything. You take them on painstakingly planned field trips and bring in esteemed guest speakers, such as successful novelists and journalists and musicians and Holocaust survivors and poets and even self-described Mark Twain enthusiasts. And they don't always appreciate or understand how much work went into that, but you don't really care, because that's not why you are doing it anyway; it was worth it if it moved them or changed them or inspired them or gave them a great outlet or memory—at least that's what you tell yourself.

They are applying to college or for scholarships, and they want you to revise their essays or write recommendations for them. They are enduring excruciating adolescence and tell you stuff in their journals that makes you their instant confidant, whether you want to be or not. They are transitioning in so many different ways. They hand you parts of their soul in a three-ring binder, and they don't always think you know, but you do. You do know. And you don't always have time to ask for advice on how to respond. You just have to go with your gut.

Sometimes you feel indignant with them, and you can't help it. You remember how at the age of thirteen when you smiled after making a mistake, you were told by a rigorous teacher that your smile was inappropriate and you needed to take yourself more seriously. And you long ago resolved that no matter how tough a day or month or year you may be having, you would never inflict that kind of hurtfulness on anyone. But then when something you said to a student comes out the wrong way, you are afraid that hurting that student is exactly what you just did. You have to realize you can't walk on eggshells with these kids, and sometimes it's just a matter of being too doggone oversensitive. (You, not them.) Sometimes they sit with you on the steps and cry to you, and you truly want to cry right along with them, because the universe is just being unfair for allowing them to have to feel that way when it's plainly obvious that they are so good, smart, and true.

Whether they show it or not, they need constant encouragement and affirmation. And some need it in different ways than others. You have to say exactly the right thing, and sometimes you don't know what to say, and you're scared they won't know how much they are cared about. You want them to see themselves the way you see them. Then you have to remember your job is not to counsel but to teach English, so you have to remain centered, balanced, and professional. You have to reel yourself back in and stay in the eye of the storm. You still must open up to them and let them know you understand them so that they will feel free to be themselves and empowered to evoke their best selves in all they do. They are sometimes testing you, though, and you can't let them get away with stuff. Sometimes you hate to have to be tough on them, but that's just the way it goes. Because it wasn't that long ago that you skipped school every now and then and tried cigarettes.

People make requests of you all day long, and you are required to follow through with every single one of them, no matter how trivial they may seem. You can't be dreamy and idealistic; you have to be practical. Teaching is fifteen jobs in one—you are manager, editor, hostess, coach, counselor, event planner, janitor, bookkeeper, secretary, and professional tissue box stocker, to name a few—and nobody understands how difficult yet thrilling it is.

And you're not even doing half the things other teachers do—the ones who coach sports three seasons or take their kids to music and robotics and dance competitions in other states. You have no idea how they do it (it's not a cliché; you are really, truly wondering), which at times can make you feel even more inadequate. In the back of your mind, you're worrying whether you are taking things too seriously or not seriously enough.

And yet. I love this job.

It has been that way for thirteen years, and I don't know how long I'll get to do this. If I ever stop wanting to teach and become burned out or disgruntled or can't bring myself to smile at anybody anymore, I will stop. I have made a promise to myself that I'll stop, for my own sake and for the sake of a future generation who deserves better.

But for right now, today, I love this job. I love this job so much. I love this job because it brings me out of myself, even when I come home kicking and screaming. I love this job even when it's stressful and unglamorous (which is every day, by the way) and at times excruciating. I love the new ideas I learn about and create in this job. I love the brilliance of my students and their discoveries and contributions. I love the eager expressions of braces-mouthed, glasses-wearing fourteen-year-olds grinning at me in the morning. And not much in this world can beat the feeling you get after calling a parent to brag about his or her daughter, especially when that student is making a positive turnaround in class. I love hearing that sigh of relief and pride in a parent's voice. It makes my day. I love the good days that come after the bad ones and how everything somehow turns out all right again.

One spring day during the last semester of my first year teaching, two graduate students from a nearby university came into my senior English class to give my students some tips on presenting their senior projects: a complex, lengthy, time-consuming graduation requirement that was the bane of their existence and mainly served as strong senioritis prevention. The two college girls who were involved seemed smart, confident, kind, and friendly. When they presented, I first acted as a facilitator, but they were doing such an effective job and I could see how well they were leading the group that I decided to sit on the sidelines, work on lesson plans, and let them essentially take charge of the class.

All I would do was look up and smile every now and then or verbalize a quick reminder to the students to listen. It was a nice break, but at the same time I felt a little jealous and left out. I mean, *I* was supposed to be the one who joked around with them best. They were *my* babies. *I* was the one who knew them and pushed them to try their hardest. The two graduate students did such a wonderful job that I suppose it was a bit like how some moms feel when their kids really like the babysitter. You're grateful and relieved they are in good hands, but it makes you feel a little hurt at the same time. It was just *a little* hard to give up my kids for a day.

After the class left, the university students gushed, "That was so much fun!" and went on and on about what a great group of students I had. They actually didn't seem like they wanted to leave. When they eventually did leave, I wanted to chuckle smugly to myself and relish my position as my class's teacher, because that's when I realized something.

Despite the clichés and complaints about high school students and teenagers being so "difficult," or moody, or even dangerous, the secret truth is that the majority of them really are *not*. The secret truth is that after just seventy minutes of being around them, you don't want to leave. Despite the occasional stress, frustration, confusion, and heartache they can cause, theirs is an awesome journey of discovery, laughter, and wonder. And I get to be a part of it every day. And I get paid (something) for it.

It's the dream seat.

BE A LEARNER AS MUCH AS YOU ARE A TEACHER

One day in about my fourth year of teaching, while revising sentences my students had written on the board, I said to my twenty-nine students, "Okay, let's see . . . everything is correct, except one word is misspelled: there is only one 'r' in the word 'embarrassed.'" I'd spelled it wrong. Then a student got out his pocket dictionary and politely pointed out to all of us the correct spelling. If I ever won a spelling bee trophy, Kanye West would be completely justified in trying to take it away from me.

I share that anecdote because as an English teacher I always love a good example of irony, and to emphasize how we can and should never stop learning, even when what we don't know can be rather embarassing . . . er, I mean, embar*rr*assing.

I know what you're thinking. Here you are, a brand-new teacher. You don't want to make any mistakes. You want to command respect, and you want to exude infallible authority, maturity, influence, and experience—although you are most likely young, inexperienced, and used to four years of being under the influence of something else. (No judgment.) But you are probably (hopefully) mature. The last thing you want is to look like you

46

don't know what you're doing. You may even have a posse of new teacher friends who are just as awesome as you are and who are trudging through it with you.

You all meet at Starbucks every Sunday afternoon to grade papers and vent and exchange advice and solve problems. You're all in it together. You've got each other's backs. But your posse can't be in that classroom with you every day. Even if you are as prepared as you possibly can be, you still are shaking in your boots. (It's okay! I won't tell anyone.)

So this may seem rather paradoxical, but my best advice to you is this: *accept that you ultimately have no idea what you are doing.* I didn't say that you haven't been *taught* or *trained* on what to do. I said that you don't know what you are doing because you don't. You can't. You have to go through some crap—some real crap—before you get an inkling of what you are doing. So let that notion seep into your psyche for a few seconds. Really understand it.

Really embrace it. Do you feel the humility yet? If not, keep saying it to yourself: *I don't know it all, I don't know it all, I don't know it all.* If you want to stay in this profession, focus not so much on being a master divine guru. Drop that act right now, and drop it fast. Instead, focus on being a learner.

Yes, that's right. Start now and never look back. Even if you just got your master's degree in education. Be a student before you are a teacher. Realize that if you are in this profession, you are going to have to be a lifelong learner in order to make it. Read, observe, listen, and learn—as much as your time and energy and family will allow. This doesn't necessarily mean you have to get an advanced degree, although that can be awesome.

When you can, attend free or inexpensive professional development seminars. Check out as many books as you can. Surf the web. Subscribe to e-newsletters. Join Facebook groups. Get on Twitter, Instagram, Pinterest, and whatever else your millennial self uses for social media these days. Get inspired. Look into some of those digital resources you will learn about at faculty meetings.

Have you heard about something called the "growth mind-set," the belief that skills and intelligence are not necessarily innate but can be developed? If not, learn more about what it is, and see what you think about it. If you are truly passionate about what you are doing—your subject, your students, your job— then nothing can hold back your curiosity or your propensity to learn.

Aim to never believe you have it all figured out. Aim to never stop growing and improving, and please don't let anyone intimidate you into thinking you can't. Just keep at it.

Even when you think you've learned it all and have reached that point where you've got things pretty much figured out, don't stop learning. I know, I know. You've heard every innovative idea, you have every useful website bookmarked under your "Favorites" tab on your school computer, you've investigated every possible way to teach irony in *Romeo and Juliet*. You've prepped for a course for five consecutive years and think that makes you an expert. But you're not.

When you close your mind, you close your heart. Boredom and unhappiness will undoubtedly follow, and that dangerous poison will reach your colleagues, students, and anyone else who knows you.

Humble yourself to learn something from everyone. Sighing or looking at the floor or your watch when someone is talking may make you seem like you're part of the "in crowd" among your teaching colleagues, but it doesn't. It just makes you look like a jerk. Treat people with respect, and that goes for students, teachers, parents, administrators, front office staff, and the custodians. Look people in the eye. Show them you want to hear and understand them. Listen to them and learn from them. Try not to be so quick to show how much you know already. Everybody can just see through it.

Now, all of that was quite preachy, wasn't it? I told you this book is ultimately advice to my new teaching self. Here's the truth: my first year of teaching, I wanted to be the one to know it all. I thought it meant power. I thought it meant control. I was wrong. When I surrendered and allowed myself to be teachable, teaching became a whole lot more enjoyable. This process didn't happen overnight.

Sometimes I didn't want to admit that I needed to reflect, tweak, and revamp. When things started to go off track—a class was getting unruly, or my teaching style and my students' learning styles weren't meshing—I didn't want to implement new ideas and strategies. But I had no other choice.

If a new method blows up in your face or is a dismal failure, that will be okay—you've weeded out a way that doesn't work. Shuck the perfectionist attitude. Try your best to be in a state of continual pondering and constant development as a teacher.

When you start to feel discouraged, seek out your encouragers. I know it's hard when you're out of time and energy, and the sun has already gone down at 5:23 on a cold February afternoon, and you have mountains of work ahead of you. And that last class of the day has literally drained every last molecule of energy you may have had left. You want to say, "Eff this. I'm movin' to Siberia." Instead, that's the time to regroup and remember to be a learner. That's the time to go talk to that veteran teacher down the hall. Who cares if he isn't as technologically astute as you are? He doesn't *want* to be. He doesn't need to be— because his students always listen to him with rapt attention, and they rise to his high expectations, too. He keeps them on their toes. Watch him to find out how. He has something to teach you, and you can't find it in a textbook or in an article that was recently posted on Twitter. And if you're having a tough day, he's got some hilarious war stories that will make you laugh and feel better. Don't rely only on yourself. Ask for someone else's guidance and wisdom about what's troubling you.

Oftentimes, this will somehow help give you the time and energy you need.

Make it a point to seek out help from your colleagues. I was sitting at a choral concert one crisp autumn evening when I saw some faculty members performing onstage with the students. All of a sudden it hit me: I was swimming in a veritable sea of professional colleagues who were insanely talented and dedicated. They could be teaching at a university any day or making a lot more money contributing their artistic talents to other organizations. But they still chose to be here, with high schoolers, no less.

And even more than that, they were really, really nice! They were willing to share their resources, expertise, knowledge, and experience. People like this are amazing. Get all the wisdom and enthusiasm you can from them. If you find someone who wants to teach you a new way to use some new software or show you how to upload a video to SchoolTube, let them. Let them show you before jumping in to tell them all *you* know. Invite them to dinner or ask them to meet you somewhere for coffee or a glass of wine. (Yes, teachers can drink wine, at least most of them. There are others who probably shouldn't.)

For me, this reaching out for help thing was not always so easy. I was kind of shy. An art teacher I once worked with named Lisa Woods always seemed perpetually harried, probably because she was always engaged in some vitally important or creative activity with her students that required hard work and long hours. She made no bones about being stressed out. I admired her but was intimidated by her, even though she seemed perfectly cordial. One winter day I went out on a limb and emailed her to see if she'd be interested in showing my creative writing class how to make journals sometime. To my pleasant surprise, she jumped at the chance, responding to my email enthusiastically with all caps and a rather notable number of exclamation points. I went down to her classroom and finally vented to her that I was struggling with some of the students we shared. She sighed and smiled.

"They're art kids," she explained. "Believe it or not, they really, really need structure. They really need to know what to expect. And they're smart as whips, and they expect you to be on your game." Then she showed me how she maintained her calendar and shared valuable secrets for how she stayed organized. We kept talking. I eventually learned the woman has won multiple awards, earned an MFA, and has a three-page-long résumé that would make Picasso blush. (That is, if it were possible for him to blush. I don't think he was ever embarrassed about much. But, then, who knows?

Anyway, the point is she is a dynamo when it comes to art.) But I realized that somewhere along the line she, too, started from a place of not knowing. She used to be a learner and still is. Everyone starts somewhere. Lisa was one of many teachers to give me new ideas. In my teacher trainings, we were advised early on to keep an "ideas" notebook or folder.

Anytime you come across a new idea or helpful information in a meeting, seminar, or class, or from a colleague, stick the handout or memo in your idea folder. It's important to discipline yourself to actually refer to and regularly *use* this folder, however, instead of just allowing it to sit there (which, unfortunately, is what I have sometimes done).

When you learn something, share it with others. Don't hoard your ideas and lessons and study guides. Give them away, pay it forward, and it will come back to you tenfold. My dear friend and former teaching colleague, Joan Lindley, let me borrow countless tangible resources, but to me, the most valuable she shared with me was the intangible resource of her experience. I felt daunted about teaching Shakespeare. She and I would meet in her kitchen or out for dinner, and she would tell me the story of *Macbeth* and *Hamlet* over pad Thai. She broke down the big picture and interjected quotes from the play into her storytelling in a way that left me riveted. And I could then go apply what I learned from her in my own classes the very next day. She taught me so many things about teaching, but sitting across from her and soaking up her passion for literature and watching her show me how to tell a story in a way that would pull in my students was what I recall most. Today that's how I aim to teach Shakespeare: I emulate Joan. I don't believe I could have found out how to do that in any of my dozens of Shakespeare books or even from expertly-taught Shakespeare seminar classes in college.

As a new teacher, I often believed that asking for help meant stealing ideas or taking credit for another person's hard work, or looking stupid. That's not what it means to ask for help. As my former ninth-grade English teacher, Mrs. Patty (who later became my mentor when I started teaching and let me cry my eyes out to her one afternoon my first year), told me one day, asking for help is a sign of confidence and strength, not weakness. So seek out and show up for that person-to- person experience of teaching and learning. Seek out a mentor who will be invested in you and care about you. Seek out several of them, if you can. *Share* your problems and questions with people you can trust. Let them teach you and show you the way. You don't have to go it alone.

SURVIVING THE HONEYMOON PERIOD
(WE CAN'T ROMANTICIZE THIS JOB)

In my first few months as a new teacher, everything was glorious. Everything was exciting and rewarding and wonderful. I had wells of energy, enthusiasm, and patience. I would get in my car to go home and blast Celine Dion's "A New Day Has Come." (Don't judge.) That first set of papers I graded was the most adorable sight I had ever laid eyes on. All of those bubble-lettered, handwritten words with hearts instead of periods, carefully crafted, I presumed, just for my eyes! This was my opportunity to influence the future, to gently nudge tomorrow's leaders toward genius by telling them how creative and brilliant and talented they all were. They laughed at my jokes and listened to my stories and did whatever I asked. This was the epitome of joy, power, and hope, and I encountered it every day. But that "honeymoon phase" was quickly over.

After a few months of exerting a reasonable amount of influence in which you haven't completely messed up too much, you will quickly realize that you have the unique position of being in a quite rewarding place of authority with your students. They smile at your every quip, listen patiently to your anecdotes, and notice every detail about you, from the pattern of your slacks to whether or not you got bangs over the weekend. In the eyes of some, you are the sun and the moon and the stars all put together. Needless to say, this can turn into one dangerous ego trip.

You start to imagine yourself as having god- like powers and you start wanting to be the "fun" teacher. You understand why there are so many movies about teaching: it's so full of drama and excitement! In your mind, you consider throwing candy bars to the students like Michelle Pfeiffer did in *Dangerous Minds* (who was playing the real LouAnne Johnson, who never actually did that because she wanted her students to be healthy), or reenacting the classical-music-playing/soccer- coaching/standing-on-desk Robin Williams in *Dead Poets Society*, or placing potted flowers around the room like Erin Gruwell from the movie *Freedom Writers*. You want to be legendary, charismatic and unforgettable like the teachers played by Denzel Washington in *The Great Debaters* or Richard Dreyfuss in *Mr. Holland's Opus*. You want to keep your class in a constant state of laughter, motivation, and inspiration, like the calculus teacher Jaime Escalante in *Stand and Deliver*.

You laugh at Cameron Diaz in *Bad Teacher*, judging her character for all the teaching mistakes *you'll* never make. You never want to be on any student's bad side because you think it means the fun and inspiration will be over. You want to do whatever you can to hold on to that good feeling of being cherished as their "favorite." And if you are an English teacher, you probably love words, literature, and stories. If you love stories, you're probably going to be very passionate. If you are very passionate, you're probably going to be very sensitive. If you are sensitive, you may tend to become disillusioned.

Please try to avoid all of that. If you start slacking and start relying on style over substance, you will fail. And although while you are failing, your adoring students will have you believing you are some invincible deity and everything you touch still turns to magic or gold, you will inevitably discover that's not the truth.

Also, in your first few weeks of teaching, you will want to share this newfound, elated feeling of importance and invincibility with everyone around you—your best friend, your mom, your sister, your grandpa, your minister, the people in your prayer group, everyone on your email list, your other best friend, your neighbors, your mail carrier, your cat.

You will believe that all of these individuals really, really care.

They don't.

Believe me, I had to accept this truth myself.

I have had to learn that I can't romanticize things. Teaching is a tough job. If it's not, I'm not working hard enough. The good news is, the real reward comes from the real hard work, not the initial euphoria and excitement I feel at the beginning of each school year. But just as with any meaningful relationship, teaching takes time, dedication, commitment, patience, and hard work.

An Average Day in My Life as a New Teacher:

In the first few weeks of my teaching career, everything seemed like it was going to be nothing but a piece of cake. *They're paying me for this?* I continually wondered.

Those were the days. I had no clue what was coming, and you won't either. But that's okay.

Here's a rough sketch of what one particular day was like for me:

6:00 AM: Jumped out of bed with a feverish start. . . .

It was a Tropicana mornin' and I couldn't wait to
go out and run three miles.
(Okay, so maybe that really happened only about
once a week.)
(Okay, maybe just once every two weeks.) (Okay,
so it was really more like once a month, all right?)

6:45–8:30 AM: Did some yoga, drank herbal tea, and had a
calm meditation period before beginning the new day.
(Again, I'll let you decide if that's true.)

6:45–8:30 AM, the real one: Okay, so it was really
more like hitting the snooze button five times until I
finally *had* to get up, catching one hard-hitting news
segment by Ann Curry on the *Today* show while
downing about two and a half cups of coffee, quickly
scrambling some eggs for breakfast, and racing around
my apartment to iron my pants in time to be ready to
leave for work. (This was back when I was fresh from
the adult corporate world; I didn't know yet that neither
students nor teachers cared if you ironed your pants.)

8:31 AM: Yay! Only 8:30! Going to make it to work ahead of
time! Where are my keys?

8:33 AM: Ahead of schedule, with time to load the
dishwasher real quick. Wonder where my keys are.

8:36 AM: Apparently not under the couch or the bed.

8:38 AM: Or anywhere on the kitchen counter.

8:39 AM: $%&^! Where are my *^%@%$ keys!? 8:40 AM:
Raced out the door with a pitiful excuse for
a bag lunch and my briefcase, which usually included
a teacher's edition textbook that I then viewed as the
pedagogical bible, as well as the perpetual mountain
of papers I had to grade. Depending on the day, my
briefcase typically weighed anywhere from sixty-five
to seventy-five pounds.

8:44 AM: Slid into work thirty seconds ahead of the time we
were officially supposed to be there.

8:46 AM: Entered mobile unit (aka trailer), turned on the five
lamps I elected to use instead of the normal overhead

lights every other teacher used. Since Mrs. C.'s classroom was the last

classroom I'd really observed, my Montessori-esque teaching philosophy back then was that fluorescent lights created an
unwelcoming environment for students, while I wanted my classroom to be a humming, nurturing womb of creativity. I was *so* wrong.
. .. The constant low lights soon only served to help my students take naps.

8:47 AM: Checked email, went into main building to sign in, checked perpetually empty mailbox; eagerly smiled as I passed all the wise, together, experienced veteran teachers in the hallway, who sometimes smiled back if they cared to bestow a greeting on me.

8:53 AM: Answered phone call from Mrs. Patty in next mobile unit over, who would check in to inquire about anything from whether or not they had fixed my printer to whether I had enough books.

8:55 AM: Carefully wrote the day's date and assignment on board for the college prep eleventh graders, my very first class of students.

8:57 AM: Chris, the cheerful quiet kid who was always early, entered.

9:00 AM: Other students, mainly comprised of students half a foot taller than me, slowly trickled in with their hi-tops and football jerseys.

9:02 AM: Busied myself with paperwork at my desk and barely looked up when they came in unless they were there to give me a late-bus pass. They had begun to get the routine of starting their journals immediately, so I basically ignored them as I tried to conceal my inner excitement that they were not skipping and were actually in my classroom on time. I also had to play it cool in order to hide how utterly thrilled I was about spending the next hour and a half with them and the miraculous joy they would unconsciously bring to my life at various intervals throughout the forthcoming class period. I had spent at least a couple of hours preparing for the next hour or so, and although I was inundated with papers to grade, I was on pins and needles to start the lesson. They never knew this, though, because I played it cool.

9:03 AM: The day's journal assignment was to write a letter to the victims of Hurricane Katrina. I looked up and almost rubbed my eyes in disbelief that Damion (yes, the name would indeed indicate some type of clue), for once, was actually writing. This was the first day I didn't have to nag him. I was in a state of minor shock. I wanted to cry with pride and happiness but didn't want to embarrass him or disrupt class so instead handed him a discreet Post-it Note that read briefly, "Damion, I am really proud of you for working hard right now. I know that you can keep up the good work—Ms. N." I felt that referring to myself by the first initial of my last name would make me seem like one of those familiar, legendary, and endearing teachers, like Mrs. C., but it only served to make it more difficult for them to remember my name.

9:10 AM: Cierra, one of the brightest and liveliest girls, was also working. A couple of weeks ago, she probably would have given her usual groan with a statement involving any of the following:

"Ms. Newlin, I can't think of anything to write."

"Ms. Newlin, I'm done." "Ms. Newlin, this is hard."

"Ms. Newlin, I don't want to do this."

She was well aware that I cared about her as if she were my daughter, but that was only until I gave my students their first pop quiz on *The Crucible*, during which Cierra practically threw a temper tantrum:

"I don't *understand* this play," she had cried in an exasperated voice punctuated by the loud slamming of her book. "I *told* you that *yesterday*."

The class stared at her, then at me for my reaction. My heart was pounding. All I could do was give her a firmly disappointed stare.

"Cierra, I'm sorry that you feel that way. But, unfortunately, taking this quiz is non-negotiable."

She sulked a second more but stopped complaining. From then on, whenever anyone complained, I would say, "I'm sorry, but it's non-negotiable."

Then the kids started to say it before I had to. Anytime anyone sulked, the rest of the class would laugh in unison: "It's non- negotiable!" So eventually all I had to say is "that is N squared" or "that is N.N." whenever they complained or gave excuses.

9:20 AM: I told the students they had two more minutes to wrap up their journal assignment. This was never an accurate timeline. I always gave them more time than I said I would. It was always really more like five minutes. I still have a problem with it. An administrator advised me to use a timer on my Smartboard with the speakers. Whenever I do that, however, I invariably set it to go off entirely too loud, and the entire class has a collective heart attack when the time is up.

9:25 AM: Gave open-book quiz on act 2 of Arthur Miller's *The Crucible* to the usual moans and groans punctuated by jokes and laughter.

When they got something right, I went crazy. I said it in a mock angry tone:

"That's exactly right, Isaiah," I would snap while beaming with pride. "How in the *world* did you get to be so smart? . . . It com*plete*ly blows my mind. You guys crack me up how you love to pretend that you're not smart when you know that you are. Who do you think you are fooling?" (I didn't know at this time that praise should be more oriented toward effort, improvement, and hard work instead of fixed qualities like being "smart." *Ding!* Your attempt at encouragement was all wrong. Try again, "Ms. N!") Then I would go back to the lesson, and they wouldn't know whether to laugh or be scared of the crazy lady. I loved to be tough on them and laugh with them and consistently praise them for every little thing they did right. Although it came as a complete surprise to them, I had seen and could quote many lines from the movie *Friday* (featuring Ice Cube and Chris Tucker) and, most importantly, I would do anything necessary to reinforce the idea that they were bright, special, and capable human beings who had what it took to achieve success.

10:00 AM: On this particular day, we might have been talking about internal/external conflict and themes. After I gave a little lecture, I would ask them to get into groups to find examples in the story and then present them to the class. They pretended to hate making these presentations, but every now and then I would see them trying to hide a smile. They seemed to secretly enjoy being the center of attention, and it kept them focused. I tried to make them get up in front of people to do presentations a lot so that they could gain practice and confidence.

10:29 AM: Shamel: Had to remind him daily to take off his do-rag (per school policy); skinny, quiet, soft-spoken, conscientious, artistic, big puppy eyes; worked the late shift at his job and was exhausted but still always tried his hardest. Sometimes at the end of class he'd come up and show me some wonderful drawing he'd made, and the kid had talent. Their rough drafts of their papers on Lorraine Hansberry's *A Raisin in the Sun* had been due the previous week, and every day Shamel kept saying he didn't have his paper and was "still working on it." I kept getting on him to bring it in and reminding him that points would be taken off for every day it was late. Well, on this day, finally, very sheepishly at the end of class as everyone was filing out, he not only handed me his lengthy, typed-up rough draft, but he had also brought in a huge collage of pictures with all the themes, characters, settings, and so on. His poster was awesome. I wanted to cry with pride.

10:30 AM: The bell rang. I would have approximately one minute to pee, because the next class was freshman honors English, and the students would be banging down the door, because although they had a full five minutes to change classes, they were freshmen and felt that they must arrive at least two hours ahead of time for everything.

10:31 AM: Twenty-four little cherubs came shuffling in with a seemingly irrepressible enthusiasm for life in general. Someone had sprinkled little bits of sunshine dust on every one of their precious little heads, and together they were the light of my life. These were the PVA (performing/visual arts) kids, the ones who were going to become star ballerinas, musicians, singers, actors, and artists. (Little did I know how much I would relish this ephemeral time of unjaded innocence because I would teach many of them again three years later when they became seniors in my AP English class. And they had become significantly less enthusiastic and irrepressible: more like ready to get out of high school and into college and away from parents. But they were still the light of my life, despite their being too mature and grown up to care.)

10:35 AM: They would all come rushing up to talk to me about something. They cared about my opinion on things and wanted to tell me things: how far they got on the previous night's reading homework, their older sister had just arrived home from college, they won their soccer game the previous night, and guess what, they had two bagels, a banana, AND a granola bar for breakfast. I couldn't wait to see how smart and talented and hardworking they would show me they were today. But again, with this class, I had to play it cool and conceal my inner joy at their presence.

10:36 AM: Gave quiz on chapters 3 and 4 of *Silas Marner*. I had gotten the wrong list of required reading for ninth graders (the book was intended for twelfth graders!), but they plowed through it anyway. I tried my best to create a more difficult quiz in order to challenge them in critical and reflective thinking, but still, I knew my little smarties would never fail me no matter how hard I tried to make it for them. Every challenge they would take on eagerly; at that time there was no task too daunting, because they were so creatively, innocently, uniquely conscientious about doing their best.

They scribbled their thoughts furiously while I leisurely graded the last of their book summaries/reflections. I knew if I didn't give them feedback soon, they would pester me about when they could expect to get their papers back, since, like being on time, they loved grades. The book summary was an idea a friend had given me when she taught English. They had to choose a book, approved by me, then write a one-page summary reflection every week on the pages they'd read for that week. The idea was to keep them reading and writing. Pretty soon I thought I was going to jump out of a window if I had to read one more word about the vampire-romance novel *Twilight*..

After I finished grading, I went around to
check their vocabulary notebooks while they were
working on their quiz and internally laughed at their
adorable attempts to use the word "vociferous" in a
sentence, although I would take great pains to
correct them so that they would continue becoming
the great geniuses they were meant to be.
Everything they did was adorable and exhibited the
strongest effort. Did I mention that?

11:00 AM: Quiz took longer than I thought. Afterward,
there was some shuffling, rearranging, minor
mischief, and chatter, usually initiated by three or
four of the class clowns, all of whom I would *never*
dare reprimand. I didn't want to disrupt a single fiber
of what I perceived as their marvelously unique
personalities and fragile confidence. Instead, all I had
to do was gently admonish them with a simple, "All
right, guys" in just the right tone, and they would
instantly become as quiet as feathers. (The technique
lasted for a good five weeks.) I thought it was
because they looked to me as their long-lost favorite
babysitter because I provided them with a haven of
acceptance, creativity, and motivation, since, as I
mentioned before, they were close to the center of
my existence.

It was now time for the *Silas Marner* trivia
game, which was marked by learning, laughter,
controlled shouting, and general fun. *Silas Marner*
was an exercise in nineteenth-century drudgery,
with its complex language and plot. So if they were
reading the classic work, I believed I owed it to
them to at least make it somewhat entertaining.
They would make up flash cards, which I
supplemented with my own, and two at a time they
would come to the board to write the answer to the
question I called out; whoever wrote the correct

answer first would win. They also had to come up with witty team names related to the book.

They had chosen the "Agnostics" (an interesting choice that totally related to the book) and the "Weavers," for their namesake school and the occupation of the title character, Silas Marner. See what I told you? Such brilliance these cutie-pie sweethearts would exhibit.

11:30 AM: Now it was serious time. I was very disturbed by the previous day's journal entry from one of the students in this class, a student I had believed to be bright, sensitive, and caring, so I was still somewhat horrified by his reply to the prompt "Write a letter to Hurricane Katrina victims": "Dear Hurricane Katrina victims, it may sound mean to say this, but guess what—you deserve it. Yes, that's right. If you didn't evacuate when they told you, then it's your own fault. Don't come crying to the government for help when you put yourself in this situation on your own."

I had been torn between accepting this as simply a written opinion from one of my most spirited students or doing something about it. After a night of thinking on it, I decided on the latter.

When the class became silent, I wrote on the board in letters the length of my arm "EMPATHY." Only five of them raised their hand when I asked if they knew what that means. We discussed both the word and how it related to the hurricane, and after about ten minutes of debate, the class had still not reached a consensus.

That's when I passed out photos I had clipped from a magazine I had bought at Barnes & Noble the previous night and gave each of the students one to study. Some of the pictures were of men paddling down the flooded streets, some were of people carrying their dogs on their shoulders as they waded through knee-deep water, some were of children wearing oxygen masks outside the Superdome. I asked them to look at the pictures and then close their eyes and picture the person they loved the most out of anyone in the entire world. Then I told them to look back at the picture and imagine it was their loved one in that picture. Now did they feel empathy? Write. I tolerated no sound but

the scribbling of pencils until the bell rang. At that time, I felt very self-satisfied and Erin- Gruwellish.

12:05 PM: Lunch never came soon enough. For the bargain of five dollars, the culinary arts teacher, Jason, would prepare lunch every day for the teachers and staff. This was so that the kids taking culinary classes could practice gourmet cooking and we could practice eating it. Jason wore a constant, winning smile, and all the teachers and students adored him. His life would be taken ten years later in a motorcycle accident. I can still see his smile in my mind, and my heart hurts. The gourmet meal was the highlight of our day. On any particular day, any culinary delight might be possible: fried chicken or perhaps a BLT sandwich with fresh, dark green lettuce and red tomatoes on whole wheat bread. I sat with the rest of the faculty and continued to try to make small talk, although I would have been too intimidated and busy to bond with any of them quite yet.

12: 45 PM: There would only be eight in my next class, eleventh-grade honors English. Myra, my star pupil, arrived early. She was a tall, sixteen-year-old beauty who loved to laugh. She had a 102 average in class and consistently worked hard. Then in came Elliott, her male counterpart. Every day Elliott greeted me with a congenial demeanor and had nothing but a conscientious and fun- loving attitude toward seemingly everything. Two years later I would see him again, working at the grocery store in my neighborhood to pay his way through college. Next was Jason: brown shaggy hair, preppy, and sweet with a constant smile, easygoing personality, and an eagerness to work hard.

Jimmy, another kid, was usually next: literate and attentive. Next would come Jeffrey and Al, polar opposites. Jeffrey was a talkative football player who always wore shades, while Al was quiet and thoughtful. Last, and almost always last, would be Carter and Maggie, with their drinks from Chick-Fil-A in hand. Carter liked to hunt and go four-wheeling and had it in his mind that he was dumb in English and should always sit in the back of class. I proved him different by giving him A's when he truly deserved them, much to his shock.

Maggie was the only one out of all my classes that for some reason I babied. I could smell cigarette smoke on her when she came in, and I knew that she worked nights and weekends at the grocery store. I presumed she was involved with a rebellious crowd at school based on her detailed recounts of her weekend events.

Maggie was all at once sarcastic, endearing, impossible, and vulnerable. I changed the thermostat whenever she asked and let her use the class blanket if she needed it. Yes, I actually had a class blanket. It was in the storage closet, and I took it home and washed it, probably just for her. I still have no idea why I did that. The kid had me wrapped around her finger.

After their journal entries and grammar worksheets (I didn't yet know any other way to get grammar lessons in), they would act out a debate between characters in act 3 of *The Crucible*. Most of them decided on staring at everybody or laughing, while Elliott and Myra were the only ones who really had a clue what they were talking about. I put my head in my hands and decided to move on to the next project. I introduced the rubric for their next essay with an ingenious assignment titled "Themes in the Play."

To elucidate even further, I would vaguely inform them that their grade would consist of 33 percent content, 33 percent conventions, 33 percent organization, and 1 percent SPICE, which is what I considered a rather witty acronym I made up all by myself when I had accidentally mispronounced "double-spaced" as "double-spiced," much to their delight. SPICE stands for Super Perfect Intelligently Creative Excellence. Not exactly a highly measurable, objective form of assessment, but, oh well.

2:30 PM: The bell would finally ring and I was done teaching for the day. The last block would be planning, which ideally meant grading, creating lesson plans, and organizing but often included meetings with other English department faculty and surfing the Internet for lesson plan ideas.

4:15 PM: The day was officially over for faculty. 4:30 PM: I would go across the street to the YMCA because I had a free membership as a faculty member.

4:30 PM: Okay, so again maybe that wasn't something I really did every day, but that, like, didn't make me a bad person.

Anywhere between 4:15 and 6:15 PM: I went home. To go back to work. Because I nearly always had work that had to be done at home.

This was the honeymoon period. Everything flowed peacefully. There was no conflict, no drama, no headaches or heartaches or tears. I had no idea of the challenges and adventures that awaited me. And you might not, either. But like I said, it will all— eventually, somehow, Divine Chaos of the Universe willing—be okay.

LISTEN TO YOUR STUDENTS
AND THEY WILL LISTEN TO YOU

Did you know that you can't cut off the thorns of a rose?
You can try, but it won't work. Ask any florist. When
florists try to cut off the thorns on roses, it makes the
flowers wilt. The thorns are just a part of their whole
makeup, the way their creator . . . well, created them.

Try as I might, I can never get rid of all of my
students' "thorns." I just can't. I can't change the argument
they had with their mom the night before, or the fact that
they're grounded, or the fact that they broke up with their
boyfriend the day before, or the fact that their dad beats
them up, or the fact that their mom is too drunk to keep their
stepdad from abusing them, or the fight on Instagram they
got into ten minutes before class with the girl who used to be
their best friend from 6th   grade and the simmering anger
they feel. I can't change their moods. I can't take away their
thorns. I may think I can, and sometimes I still try, but I just
can't do it. All I can really do is provide those "roses" with
the sunlight and nourishment they need so that they can
thrive, and before long, I don't notice the thorns so much.

As teachers, we can choose to focus on the roses or the thorns. When it comes to students, I have to focus on all the things I love about them, because there is a lot to love. When I am slightly attuned to their mood, whether it's attentive, lethargic, sullen, cheerful, or talkative, it makes life a lot easier in the long run.

We want to listen to our students because we ultimately want our students to talk, to respond to us. And we have to create a space where they want to do that. I try to create that safe, secure space for my students. I try not to get frustrated when my students ask questions that I've answered seemingly a hundred times already. I tell them, "The only dumb question is the one that's never asked." Even as adults we sometimes don't ask questions for fear of looking dumb. It's not that much different for kids.

I've also learned the hard way that my students don't always respond the way I expect or believe they should. And I am oftentimes powerless whether a student responds to me positively or not, and I have to give them space for that, too. My first year teaching middle school, I was talked into being the assistant coach for the Junior Varsity girls' basketball team. Now I might be tall, and basketball is definitely in my genes, but my natural skill is pretty much nonexistent, to say the least. Nevertheless, I accepted the position, believing the head coach when he told me it would be a great way to connect with the students. A tall man in his 50s who reminded me of Samuel L. Jackson in the 2005 movie *Coach Carter*, he had decades of playing and coaching experience, and he knew his stuff. The team adored him.

"You have to practice, practice, and practice some more," Coach would tell them, "whether I'm checking up on you or not. And if you're not practicing, it will show. What's done in the dark will come to the light."

I started cramming as much as I could glean from books like "Coaching Youth Basketball For Dummies," but to no avail. I hated being a coach. I didn't know what I was doing. During practices, I didn't have much of a purpose except to help get balls that went off the court and yell out an occasional, "That's the ticket, Jordan! Nice shot! Woo-hoo! You go, girl!"

One 7th grader, Amanda, and I did not get along from just about day one. She was spunky, smart, and adorable. I didn't understand why she didn't like me. She would glare at me and ask me to do mundane things like pick up a sweaty towel off the court during a game. I felt she should give me more respect, seeing as I was "Coach Newlin" and all. So after one too many times that she ignored a directive I gave, I proceeded to take her out in the hallway while the rest of the girls practiced in the gym. I reamed her for at least 20 minutes on her "attitude" and how she needed to respect me more, insisting that she have a "team player" mentality. I was projecting all my feelings of purposeless powerlessness onto her. I took my own insecurity out on a seventh grader who was almost half my size. I was, of course, very wrong, but in that moment, on that dark February evening, I felt so justified. But what I said and did came to the light, and her parents emailed the Athletic Director to complain about me. I felt demoralized and humiliated; in my eight years of teaching, this would be the second complaint a parent had ever made about me. A year passed, and she went into eighth grade. (Her parents undoubtedly had made sure she didn't get me as her teacher.) She ignored me whenever we passed in the hall. With each passing day, her height grew, and so did my feelings of shame about my behavior the previous school year. I talked to confidantes about this nagging guilt I still felt and what to do about it, and I even wrote her a letter of apology and burned it in my backyard fire pit, hoping the atonement would be received by the universe.

One fall morning Amanda was on her way from music class to math class, and I was coming out of the library. I was having a productive morning. Plus, my skirt matched my shirt, and I was having a good hair day. With my coffee mug in hand, I walked gently alongside her. It was time, something inside told me. So I decided to take my chances and gently say, "Hey, Amanda? Can I tell you something really quick?" and when I did, she continued walking, but nodded ever so slightly.

I continued walking alongside her and said quietly, "I just want you to know that last year, I was wrong in how I talked to you and treated you. I wish I could go back and change it, but I can't. So I'm sorry. I just wanted you to know that." A glimmer of not unpleased surprise flashed in her eyes—just for a second. "Okay," she replied and kept walking on ahead of me. To me that was progress. No matter what she did or how she felt from that point on, I was able to let it go. I'd done all I could do. Nothing changed much. She still ignored me. At the end of the school year, I seconded a colleague's nomination that she receive one of the top awards on eighth grade graduation day. Then on her last day of eighth grade, she came up to me. "Coach Newlin, will you sign my yearbook?" I held back my shocked delight and gave her a big smile. "Of course! I'd be honored."

Maybe I should never have apologized, another teacher might argue, and for them, that's their truth. But when it comes to dealing with my students, I have learned I have to adhere to *my* truth, not what someone else thinks are how things "should" be.

For example, one of the things I struggle with lately as a teacher is adhering to tightly defined learning goals. In my classroom, sometimes the learning process doesn't follow a straight line; instead, it goes in different directions. I wish I reserved more room in my lesson plans just for "time to listen to students." And I wish I reserved more time for the random "teachable moments" that pop up for me all the time when I'm teaching a concept, and I just *have* to tell that anecdote, or reference the news event that just occurred that morning, or play that particular song or excerpt from a TV show to help illustrate a point. Oftentimes my students want to chime in with their own points, and I feel it is my educational duty to allow room and time for that.

I think learning about literature, language, and communication mirrors the human condition. Sometimes, the most effective and meaningful discussions have a central focus but can often go off topic; one idea leads to another, and new, unexpected connections and insights develop.

Sometimes the student is the one who gives the teacher a new insight, and it can be simple but unforgettable. For example, one year my students Carlos, Miguel, Ana, Juan, Estefania, and Gerardo didn't speak English as their first language, and I didn't speak Spanish as my first language. So when I taught them what their vocabulary word "valiant" meant, they taught me that the word *valiente* has a similar meaning—brave. It was a win-win situation.
Students will let us know their favorite songs and TV shows, what they're into, what they hate. We just have to make time to listen.

If my students and I start to experience a disconnect from the subject and each other, there is a high likelihood that I've stopped listening to them, and they start to see my class as offering no incentive besides a test score that carries little meaning other than ensuring their entry to the next grade or course level. My class becomes a dead zone when I allow this to happen--- when I allow whatever pressure I think I'm under to take over our humanity, our innovative creativity, our shared laughter and respect. Now undoubtedly, there are skills and concepts related to language and literature that every student should know, but some skills I teach won't be tested on a multiple choice exam: skills like presenting an original poem with self-confidence, being an "up stander" instead of a bystander when they see bullying occur, practicing compassion for themselves and for others, collaborating to solve problems, and even how to give a meaningful apology.

Some teachers, of course, adopt a fundamentally different view, and I understand and respect that. They might argue, "It's *my* classroom, and I'm not here to be their mama. I am here to teach them concepts, facts, and skills.

I'm the boss in here, and what I say goes. I don't give two cents about their *'feelings.'''* That's absolutely fine for those teachers, but it didn't work for me when I tried it in my first year teaching, or any year after that, for that matter. I believe that nine times out of ten, *being a dictator in a classroom really doesn't work.* If I have to resort to that strategy, it means *I've* lost, not my students. Today we live in a different world than people did a generation ago. The world of teachers and education has completely transformed. We live in a democracy where our youth are encouraged to use their voices. What worked back then doesn't necessarily work now. It's oftentimes futile to "lay down the law" and "show 'em who is boss."

Kids are intuitive. No matter how smart and equipped we may be, they know when a teacher is new and clueless. Trying to mask an inherent powerlessness with a pretentious, domineering façade won't impress or motivate them. Any time I've tried that, it usually isn't sustainable. I've never been able to keep up the act. Like, I'll demand angrily that the room become "completely quiet," and right after that, I will end up tripping over a cord in the middle of the classroom. It's possible for a teacher to temporarily force self-confidence, but everyone, including the teacher, is most likely going to be miserable. The battle may be won, but the war is lost. In my experience, my students and I have more growth and success when I choose to tweak and adjust, not force or coerce. I can choose to break down in tears at the end of every day, or I can choose to swallow my pride and listen to my students instead of my ego.

One fall my seventh year of teaching, I had a class of 29 freshmen who were the bane of my teaching existence. The class was marked by the kind of subtly morbid atmosphere that you can never quite put your finger on; it's just when something is completely off kilter and creates an ominous sense of dread. Think "Anyone, anyone? Bueller?" but not in a way that's meant to be funny. When I was giving instruction in this particular class, the students all either

73

looked at me like they were smelling a can of expired sardines, talked while I was talking, or outright ignored me. I vented about them to trusted friends, calling them "the Bratistas." It was a label I could conveniently use to dismiss and disconnect from them, to put myself above them. The Bratistas seemed to know everything and display nothing but utter confidence in themselves, and they seemed impossible to motivate or reach in any meaningful way. I had never taught a class that made me feel so...*unneeded*.

One day, I collected their journals. An especially exemplary Bratista, Janet, had written me a note in her journal: "I am so sick of this class and your ridiculous teaching style. This class is so boring and dumb. Go to some diciplin [sic] classes. Learn how to control your students. You need to learn how to get a backbone." Well, gosh, tell me how you *really* feel next time, Janet. Sheesh! The class eventually made me question whether or not I was truly meant for the job (and it wouldn't be the first time I questioned such a thing.) When the semester was finally over and the last Bratista shuffled out of my class on the last day, I breathed a sigh of relief that was plausibly heard all the way to the cafeteria on the other side of campus. They were gone. Finally! The constant hangnail-like discomfort of the past four months with them was over.

The following fall, after a long and relaxing summer break, I was excited about a clean slate. I took an eager look at my roster for my tenth-grade class. It would undoubtedly be a whole new crop of students to look forward to: yippee! Instead, my mouth dropped and my heart sank when I perused the list: nearly every single one of *their* names was on the roster. The Bratistas!? *Again?* What the heck? How? Why? What made it necessary for the divine chaos of the universe to force me to trudge back through another level of purgatory I'd already endured? Why were the gods punishing me?

So in the week before school began, I furiously went to work as best as I could, preparing for another round of slow hell. I spent hours upon hours creating a huge

presentation and burned up the copier with 29 copies of a
10-page packet full of rules upon expectations upon
procedures upon guidelines upon "dos and don'ts" upon
consequences. And on the first day of class, the Bratistas,
who were now *sophomore* Bratistas with even *more* reason to
believe they knew everything, looked at the packet, looked at
each other, sighed, and promptly ignored everything I said.
As we tried to get through the first couple of weeks of school
together, things got even worse than they had been their
freshman year. Two students, Ellie and Jada, would come
into class at least a full two minutes after the bell rang, with
their headphones on full blast, dancing their way into the
class with utter disregard for whom they might be disturbing,
each with one hand on her hip and one hand behind her
head, each shaking her hips back and forth, dramatically
sashaying her way to her seat. At my every request, and in no
matter how calm and polite a tone I could muster, they
huffed, puffed, and nearly blew me down. Ellie and Jada
ruled the class, not me, and everybody knew it. One day I
finally lost it and raised my voice in a tone that must have
sounded much like the villain sea monster Ursula toward the
end of *The Little Mermaid*.

Not surprisingly, raising my voice didn't work,
either. Finally, one day, in the middle of a particularly chaotic
class discussion on the novel *Siddhartha*, I stopped
instruction, told them to close their books, and take out a
sheet of paper and pencil. I had them write a timed essay on
the topic of something along the lines of "Why I should
listen to my teacher and believe she knows everything and
why I deserve to write a long difficult essay as punishment
for being rude and disrespectful." That was not the exact
topic I gave them, of course, but it might as well have been.

At the end of class, Courtney, one of the more
pensive students in the class, came up to me, practically
shaking.

"Can I have that book back that I loaned to you the other week?" she snapped. "Because if you're not going to read it, I know someone who will!"

My eyes widened, and I was so surprised I didn't know what to say. I found the book on my bookshelf, gave it to her, looked at her quizzically, then said defensively, "Courtney, I'm sorry I haven't had time to read it yet; I've just been incredibly busy this year, and--"

She cut me off. "You don't even *know* what my life is like, okay?" she shouted as she started marching out the door. "You have no *idea* what I'm going through right now!"

I took a deep breath and let her stomp out, although I was still confused. I then sat down to read the timed essays and started with Courtney's. My mouth dropped open after the first paragraph of her prose. In a thinly disguised allegory of a teacher named "Mr. Gerbee" who has no control over his classroom and punishes the class as a whole instead of looking at himself as the problem, she had subtly, brilliantly derided my futile attempt to gain authority in class that day.

She happened to come by during lunch the next day, and I asked if I could talk to her.

"So, I read your essay," I began. "And I'm willing to listen to what you have to say. If you have any insight into what I'm doing in class that might not be working, I'm open... to hearing your... thoughts."

Her manner softened, and she took a deep breath.

"Ms. Newlin," she said, in the tone of a doctor giving a patient a diagnosis that was tough, but not dire, "We need to have a...an *intervention*." She looked at me squarely, with an expression of both authority and hope.

"An intervention," I repeated, folding my arms across my chest and leaning back in my chair. "Tell me more."

She explained to me that the class as whole felt stifled by all my new rules and expectations and procedures. "I mean," she explained, "It's just that you kinda sit up there at your lectern like you think you're the queen of us. You don't give us any *choice* in anything. You just give us *work*. And those long unit packets? We *hate* those packets! It's like you're trying to…be somebody you're not." She started walking back and forth, moving her arms dramatically as she talked. The class hated all the superfluous homework and paperwork I gave them, Courtney explained, and nobody found much meaning in the assignments. She concluded, "So what we need to do, Ms. Newlin, is we need to have an intervention. We need to just sit in a circle and let everyone just get it all out."

I went to bed that night and cried my eyes out. I had been wrong. All my hours of preparation, and all of my attempts to control the uncontrollable, had failed. I could only look at myself and my own failings. I would have to give them the control. But it was control they seemed to already have! I had tried everything else; all that was left was to take off the mask. So the following day, that's what we all did.

When they walked in and saw the chairs arranged in a circle, they looked nervous and slightly disturbed. In the circle, I opened by telling them about my frustrations: with them and myself, and my dashed hopes for our class. They took turns talking about the ways our class was at times working, but mostly not, for them. They missed how we had pored through *To Kill a Mockingbird* together more slowly when they were freshmen, but now with *Antigone* and other more complex works of world literature, they felt lost, that everything was moving too fast. "But that's why you have the packets to help you collaborate and find out information for yourselves," I argued.

One of them interrupted: "The packets? The *packets*? Don't even get me *started* on the packets!" "And can we please bring back A.M. Pages?" another one asked. "That was like…my therapy." A.M. Pages had been 15 minutes of free-writing time at the beginning of class. They had been allowed to write about anything, as long as they kept their pencils moving. I never realized how much they'd gotten out of something so simple.

Believe it or not, as the "intervention" continued, and it took almost the entire class period, our big discussion did not turn out to be one long tirade against me. In fact, it was quite the opposite. It was healing. It was honest. And it was productive. They all started to share their ideas about how we could have more cross-curricular connections in class and more hands-on projects. We decided to have international celebrations at the end of each piece of World Literature we studied. Janet had the idea of bringing in food. So the following Friday we had our first celebration, and that sparked even more creative pursuits. We even went to restaurants and art galleries to write. And yes, we brought back A.M. Pages. By the next week, Ellie and Jada started coming to class on time--still dancing, mind you-- but on time. And I realized it was okay for them to dance into class. I gave them space to dance, and it made all the difference. Then one day, Jada came up behind me and put her arms around me for an impromptu hug. The following year, when she found out I was going to be moving to another city, I saw her in the school lobby, and she said, "Nah, I ain't talkin' to you. I'm mad at you. You were supposed to be my teacher my senior year. So I'm mad at you."

If I had "stayed the course" that semester and insisted upon "my way or the highway," I would not have only been wrong, I would have missed out on what turned out to be some amazing memories and a class that I now consider not Bratistas, but one of the most exceptionally talented group of young people I've ever had the privilege of teaching. It all came from listening. A few of them have friended me on social media, so I can keep up with them and see how they are changing the world in all sorts of triumphant ways that can give us all great hope for the future.

Listening to my students requires all of my senses and faculties, not just my ears.

One day, one of my brightest students, Tanesha, came to class and, non-habitually, didn't make eye contact or say hello. "Hey, you okay?" I asked. She just shrugged and walked over to her desk. She was typically attentive, on task, cheerful, and eager to learn. I kept looking at her as we began the lesson, but I couldn't catch her eye. Finally, I asked her to step out into the hallway.

"So you're not yourself today," I began. "What's goin' on with you? What is it?"

She just shook her head as the tears started rushing down her face.

"My cousin got killed last night," she stammered. She didn't have to get out any more words before I asked her if she needed a hug, andwhen she nodded, I swooped her into my arms and let her tears fall. I went inside the class, got the box of tissues and her work, and let her work out in the hall and write about how she was feeling. When I checked my email later that day, she told me that her cousin had been shot over drugs, and she was especially upset because he was only 27 and had been trying to turn his life around for his kids. "I think I will be ok," she wrote at the end of her note, "and thanks for your concern and being here for me. I really enjoy having you as a teacher because you're always going to be here for me. Love you lots, Ms. Newlin."

That felt like successful teaching. But I've had countless moments where I never took the time to take a student aside like that to see what might be going on. I just assumed a student was being lazy or moody and reprimanded that student or called the office--anything besides really listen and dig a bit deeper into what was really going on. Those were mistakes on my part. I was wrong, but it's not too late. I get another chance today, and the day after that, and the day after that. There are always new chances to keep listening.

These are my basic top 12 ways to listen as a teacher:

1. Read your students' writing and make personalized comments about what they're *saying* (not just a correction of the grammatical errors they've made.)

2. On the first day of class, send home a questionnaire for parents to complete about their children's personalities, learning styles, and other useful ways you can help them learn and grow.

3. Avoid zoning out or getting papers graded while students are sharing something in class or trying to tell you something important to them.

4. Don't let any joke at their expense slide.

5. Pay attention to their signals of boredom, anxiety, frustration, or irritation. Reflect on what it might mean and act accordingly.

6. Lead meaningful class discussions and call each student out by name to get everybody involved.

7. Find ways to make all students feel proud and worthy. Give them cards on their birthday. Brag about them to the class for who they *are*, not always just what they *do* or accomplish.

8. Really look at your students when they are speaking and try to genuinely picture what they are saying.. Put distractors (papers, computer, pencils, handouts, etc.) aside.

9. Whenever you can, attend their recitals, performances, sports games, etc. Look at who they are, and watch what they can do. You'll see them in a different light.

10. Give them some space and quiet time to think when they need it. Don't push.

11. Ask for their feedback regularly. Ask them to give you a detailed "grade" for you as their teacher, and let their responses be anonymous.

12. Immediately apologize when you've made a mistake. It sucks to be wrong, but a sincere apology can help make things right.

One of my most memorable students during my three-year stint teaching eighth grade was an absolute ball of fire. Elsa was Latina, not more than five feet tall, and a pro at snapping her finger in a circle. She often made me have to bite my lip really hard so that she wouldn't see me laugh. I did my best to keep her in check, but we all loved her to pieces. She wanted to be thirty instead of thirteen, and the rest of the eighth grade simultaneously worshipped, pitied, and feared her. She was easily upset, so one way I tried to get her to calm down was to ask her to write out her emotions, and then I would write her back.

This is one such exchange we had:

Im so mad b/cuz ms. Chadworth is tripping I aint doin nothing to her and she making me mad I dont like her at all

Elsa,
I'm sorry you are mad. Ms. Chadworth is actually a really nice and fun teacher. She tries her best to do a good job, and she takes being a teacher very seriously. She cares about all of her students. It's her job. Rules are in place because they are meant to benefit everyone. Rules are in the best interest of everyone. Ms. Chadworth just has to make sure you follow rules. I don't always like certain rules, either. For example, on my way to school, why do I have to drive 65 miles per hour? I'd rather drive 70 miles per hour. But if I do, a cop will give me a speeding ticket, and I'll have to pay at least $200. That's not how I want to spend my money. So I have to follow the rules. Rules are usually in my own best

interest, and yours, too. You'll be happier in the long run
if you follow the rules.
—Ms. Newlin

is u trying 2 b funny b/cuz i aint laughing well i dnt like
her she b triping way 2 much and I dnt like that

What do you mean by "tripping"? Why does it make you so mad?

She thinks I have gum wen I didnt she believe my sister
over me and she always be bosing me around she aint
my mom

Why does being bossed around bother you so much? Tell
me more about how that makes you feel.

I hate ppl telling me wat to do I only have one
mom and it aint her so she need to chill out or
stay away from crack. and she needs to chill
b/cuz she aint nothing 2 me all she is a stupid
teacher

What about you? How does being bossed around make
you feel? Without telling me more about your opinion of
Ms. Chadworth (I'm clear on what you think), tell me
more about you.

Well ok I hate ppl tellin gme wat to do like I said
it makes me feel like a dam slave and i dnt see no
ugly rags on me. I just dnt like it.

So if someone asks you to follow the rules, you feel like
they are treating you like a slave. When people tell you
what to do, what are you most afraid of?

I aint afraid of nothing I have nothing 2 fear
everyone who boses me around.

The days didn't always go like this. Sometimes speaking to her like an annoying psychotherapist didn't work. I lost my patience with Elsa; some days I had to send her to in-school suspension. I would try to show how tough I was and discipline her, and she would just smirk at me. She challenged me in other ways too. One day I had pulled a lesson out of my . . . uh, socks, and she was the only one who noticed. She raised her hand in the middle of my lecture on a random short story from the textbook and asked, "Um . . . what are we doing right now? What exactly are we supposed to be learning?" It was a great question. I wasn't so sure myself. She wanted to be challenged.

So if you ever encounter a student like this, who challenges *you* in every way, hang in there and have faith, because it's worth it. A couple of years after she left my class, Elsa dropped out. She called me at school one day to let me know how she had been doing and about some of the battles she'd been fighting, which I had never truly understood when she was in my class. "You never gave up on me," she said. "No matter how sassy and rude I got, you still cared about me." The following afternoon I took my baby daughter to visit Elsa at the restaurant where she worked, and she insisted on paying for our meal. She took a break from her shift, and we talked and talked. I was so incredibly proud of her. There were a few tears but a lot more laughter. Her courage and strength inspired me. It was one of the most meaningful afternoons of my life. And to this day, she still emails me to tell me that she's gotten married, or is expecting a baby. It's always a bright spot in the day to see her name pop up in my inbox just to say hello.

I once had another student named David who was a complete pain in my . . . foot. He was only five feet tall but had the power of a giant in my classroom. He got this power by snoring loudly in class, distracting the female students with excessive flirting, and generally undermining me in subtle and overt ways. "Kick him out of class!" advised a veteran teacher.

"Just say, 'See ya, Dave!'" But I didn't quite see that option having a positive outcome.

David hated *The Crucible* and *The Scarlet Letter*. He wanted to get right to Kurt Vonnegut and didn't understand why we had to mess around with the "Dear God, why is this so boring?" archaic literature I had carefully chosen for the AP syllabus. Then when we read *Catcher in the Rye*, he changed. Actually, David reminded me so much of Holden Caulfield it was uncanny. Ironically (or maybe not so ironically), he told me it was his favorite book of all time. He rarely got excited about literature analysis, but he was a huge contributor to our class discussions on that novel. He loved talking and writing about it and had great insights about what made the book meaningful and what made the characters tick. When I started asking him questions and listening to his answers, he opened up, and his behavior started changing. He became a delight.

I think it comes down to this. As a teacher I hold this tremendous power right here in my hands. How will I use it? Force them, mock them, dismiss them, belittle them, hurt their feelings, and shrug it off because they are the students and I am the teacher and that's how it should be? I have the option to do that. Will I be right? Yes. Will I whip them into shape? Yes. Who will feel good? Who will win? Usually not me. Not them. Nobody. The result is that I'll look and feel like a fool, they'll resent me, I'll resent my job, and ultimately I'll resent them. And it just doesn't have to be that way.

I must listen to my students before they will ever listen to me. There was one point in the first few months of teaching that I would literally sit at my desk and cry after one afternoon class of eleventh graders left for the day. Why did they not listen? Why did they not do as I asked? Why were they acting so lazy? Why did they not take this class seriously? I begged, yelled, pleaded, or sent them to the office. None of it worked.

I finally realized the answer to why they acted that way. Teenagers are simply living in a different world. Similar to toddlers, teenagers are learning who they are and trying to discover their own identities, separate from their adult caregivers. They have no clue about your wanting to make a difference. They couldn't care less that you want to "save" them. (And most of them could do without our "saving," thank you very much.) They don't get why you are there. All they feel is controlled and stifled when they come to school, and you are the easiest target. Your demonstration of how much they get to you—by yelling, belittling, forcing—makes it even easier. So you have to show them something different.

After my first semester, when I got a whole new crop of classes at the semester change in January, I tried something different. I decided as much as possible to completely take my ego out of the equation. I didn't focus a lot on me or on them, but instead tried to totally focus on the material as much as possible. I appreciate literature and writing, and I enjoy showing kids how to appreciate it too, or to appreciate it a little more. I try to show how excited I am about what I'm teaching. And on a good day, that gets them excited, too, which often eliminates their misbehavior.

You might find that sometimes when they are acting up, all kids really need is a simple smile from you, or perhaps some attention, a genuine kind word, or even for you to leave them the heck alone. Some of them are going through unfathomable challenges that we will never, ever know about. And despite all they are going through, *they still show up*. Be grateful that they are there, even if only with their head on their desk because they worked after school and stayed up until 1:00 AM doing homework. Instead of viewing them as lazy, consider just saying, "I'm so glad you're here. I'm glad you came to class today."

Maybe that's being a pushover, or too nice. *We can't baby them; we have to toughen them up for the real world,* some may say. Really? Is that how we treat adults in the real world, like workhorses? Why do children not deserve a break every now and then? They're experiencing growing pains, literally. Their

85

brains and bodies are still growing, and that can be really doggone exhausting. That doesn't mean letting everything slide and lowering your expectations. It means pausing for a second to put yourself in their shoes. Just one second. You will see what they want. They just want your attention. They want you to smile and lighten up. They want you to see something special in them and to believe in them, even if they don't show it. Just *laugh* with them every now and then. Have a sense of humor. You will enjoy the heck out of yourself if you can learn to let them make you laugh. When I asked them for feedback at the end of my first year, one of my freshmen wrote, "My favorite thing about this class was how easy it was to make you smile."

Please try not to believe what other people might say about how you should never smile in front of the kids until Christmas. Many of them need your smile so desperately. I tell my freshmen all the time that they are the light of my life. I tell them this because it's true and because they need to hear it.

I believe my students also need to hear regularly that no matter how different they are from one another, my classroom is a safe space for them in every way, where no one is going to make them feel dumb or worthless or put down or left out. I don't tolerate name calling or even the phrase "shut up." That may sound like an elementary school teacher, but the phrase "shut up" is just as detrimental to a sixteen-year-old as it is to a five-year- old. I am vigilant, maybe at times, too vigilant. But it's that important to me. I hope you will do the same. If you don't think it's a big deal and that "kids will be kids," the 2011 documentary *Bully* will wake you up and make you want to take action. When you see or hear any form of disrespect, teasing, or bullying, you have to nip it in the bud right away. You have to confront the student(s) and take disciplinary action if necessary. When you see a student come to school in the morning with a black eye, you have to question her and try to get the truth out of her, get to the bottom of why and how it got there, and report it to the school counselor immediately. In fact, such reporting is the law. If a student writes or says threatening things about himself or somebody else, it's also a time to contact the counselor.

You have to humble yourself. You have to open yourself up enough to listen, and doing that can be painful and awkward at times. Sometimes you will misunderstand or get some things wrong. But that still doesn't excuse you from trying. When all is said and done, you will see that your efforts have paid off. There is nothing better than the care you feel for these kids and earning their respect, or having them throw you a surprise birthday party or baby shower, or make you a class scrapbook with poems they each wrote for you, or having them say you are the best English teacher they ever had; or that you are their favorite teacher; or that, you know what, you really made them think in this class; or that they appreciate how you listened to what they said and really challenged them. Or when they come back into your room to visit and excitedly exclaim, "It still *smells* the same!" (Which I choose to take as a compliment.)

While writing this book, I wanted to see whether my efforts to listen had paid off with any of my students. I wanted to give you some evidence that if we choose patience, humility, and flexibility over blindly plowing forward, it can actually make a more lasting impact in the long run. So I reached out to former students with whom I keep up with on social media with the question: "What do you remember about my class? What do you remember about my teaching style? You can be honest!" and I was affirmed by the response.

With her permission, one of my former students, Kat Roesel, recalls my class this way:

"I remember your class being a lot of fun and engaging, and compared to a few other teachers I had during those years, you were like a breath of fresh air ("Finally, Newlin's class!"). I don't remember feeling stressed or looked down on, but raised up by how kind and supportive you were. You were in a position of authority but it felt as if we were all on a team -with- you rather than you running the class as a taskmaster . . . which may explain why (at least in my class, harhar) you were occasionally "bullied" into taking the class outside or skipping some instruction time. And of course you went to bat for me after the Senior Project fiasco, like a mama lion, and that is forever going to be one of those memories that brings me to happy- tears. You encouraged me to love writing, and I do—even the really gross, tedious research papers (Oh gods, the research papers . . .). I was able to go into university confident in my work, and take criticism without bursting into tears. And as a person, I feel like your jovial demeanor rubbed off more than this goth chick is willing to admit."

Another student, Madeline Parrish, wrote:

"This is what I always remember when I think of you as my teacher. A few of my friends were taking your creative writing class and I wasn't for some reason and was sad about it. So I did a few of the assignments my friends told me about and one day after lunch I brought you one. You looked at it, beamed, and presented it to the class filing into the room. I was a little embarrassed but I always remember the confidence you had in me. Thanks for teaching me how to be a good writer so I can face all the speeches I have to give in Japan!"

Another former student, Janke Seltsam, told me,
"When people ask me about 'my favorite teacher' I think of you. And the way you trusted me as a young adult to be myself. . . . I'm thankful for a teacher who

embraced me and didn't try to change me. That is a rarity."

Another student, Hannah Pope, recalled,

"What I really remember about your teaching style was how caring you were about everything. You were always so positive and encouraging even when we were not the easiest group to teach. I also remember you were a very warm person, and genuinely invested in us. That feeling was evident in your lesson plans and feedback, and I always appreciated it."

Receiving this feedback from former students who are now adults was a refreshing surprise. Each of them is accomplished in their own wonderful way. I think of every one of these students' faces and remember them vividly in my class. My heart would always beat just a bit faster before they came in the classroom because I knew I would have to be "on" and that they expected a lot out of me. I knew they were working really hard and were holding me up to the same high expectations they had for themselves. I did not realize at the time that I was having this impact. When you receive uplifting feedback like this from current or former students (and you will), my advice is to keep it in something my first principal called a "Smile File." These are all the little notes—simple, mind-blowing, or otherwise, from students, colleagues, and anyone else related to your teaching career—that you can take out on a gray day when you can't find your internal compass of kindness and compassion, when you think you've "blown it" with a particular student or class and things can't be repaired.

When you speak to and with your students, remember that one day (sooner than you realize, actually) they *will be* adults. Maya Angelou said, "People will forget what you said. People will forget what you did. But people will never forget how you made them feel." When you remember what is really important—listening, connecting, caring—all the other crap you had to put up with fades away. There is nothing greater than the feeling that you've actually made a positive difference, and it will be yours over and over again the longer you hang in there. Keep chugging up the mountain and focus on who you can help today. Ignore the voices (internal or external) that tell you that you can't, and believe the ones who tell you that you can. Because when you do keep listening to your students—whether they tell you what you want to hear or what you don't want to hear— sooner or later, teaching will feel like a song.

THE "COMPARISONITIS" CURE

In each school where I have taught, there are always plenty of accomplished, masterful, brilliant educators from whom it is a perpetual challenge for our school to choose only one "Teacher of the Year." After fourteen years, I am still filled with admiration for them, and occasionally a little intimidation too. I am told what these fabulous teachers do and how they do it on a regular basis: how they grade, how much homework they assign, what they do and don't put up with, what they said, what they did, what color shoes they happen to be wearing. I am told this information either by administrators at faculty meetings, the teachers themselves, by my students who compare me to them, by parents who compare me to them, or by others who indirectly suggest and wonder why I don't and can't be, think, or do it like them.

  One day one of my seniors offered a witty quip that another teacher had said about turning work in late, and he wondered aloud why I couldn't adopt the same philosophy.

  "Would you please stop comparing me to Mrs. So-and-So?" I replied in what I meant as a good-natured way.

"We are different, and you guys are just going to have to accept it!"

"Ha!" he retorted. "*Compare* you? There *is* no comparison. That's like comparing you to Gandhi. You're not even in the same league."

The sting came out of nowhere. After a millisecond of shock at his insult, I masked the inferiority panic mode I was in and quipped with a brilliant, "Well, gee, thanks!"

But his words stuck with me the rest of the day, week, and month. It took me time and building my own strong track record to choose to believe that his insult was his *opinion* and not a fact. I had to choose to believe a different truth. *I* get to decide which league I'm in. No one else does.

I am good at what I do, but I don't have it all figured out. Like all teachers, I have my issues with control, perfectionism, and a few flailing moments of emotional instability and ignorance. I am not the Buddha of adolescent psychology, and I don't know everything there is to know about the British Romantic poets. I haven't been a teacher for thirty years. I don't have a Ph.D. in education.

It may sound selfish, it may sound lazy, but I *don't* know the mother's maiden name of every single one of my students, and I *don't* arrive at work every day an hour early. I have stopped bringing back souvenirs from Hawaii for my students and baking them muffins (yes, I actually did that), and I have stopped spending every free waking hour grading compositions and papers (I'll explain why later.)

Perhaps someday I will do and be all those wonderful things and claim the title of "World's Most Dedicated Teacher." But for the moment, I just can't. And in truth, I won't. Not now. My sanity won't allow it.

I have an average to high sense of literacy, flexibility, patience, self-esteem, intelligence, occasional propensity for making my students laugh, creativity, and enthusiasm. I also pride myself on being well-hydrated, and I have always been a pretty good speller.

That is basically all I have to offer—that and fourteen years of fresh, jumbled, tripping, messy experience as an English teacher, which I would not trade for anything. All I have to offer is what I see and feel, and I can sometimes get a little too excited about sharing it. I am absolutely, completely, and unequivocally a seeker.

I don't think only certain people can understand literature. I think we were all born with a tongue, hands, and eyes and meant to communicate with each other. I believe literature can be a genuine joy for anyone. I have come to relish it about fifteen bazillion times more since I began teaching it. And there are fifteen bazillion things related to the study of English that I don't and never can know.

In the back of my mind, I often wonder about getting fired, not with a sense of panic but with a sense of logic, because one never knows in this teaching day and age. It could be the fact that I took my students outside, told them to run down the hill, then back up the hill, then write a poem about it. One of their parents is bound to call and complain that I neglected to remember his child has a severe pollen allergy. Or it could be one of my thinly veiled commentaries on a social injustice that does it, or it could be my failure to turn in a form on time.

Whatever it is, I've learned that I will be okay. I've learned to be okay with who I am as a teacher, and the reason I am okay is that I know I'm constantly striving to do it better. Someday when I am fifty, I will admit that I hope to be a female version of Robin Williams in *Dead Poets Society*. There, I said it. I want to be that ingenious, that fearless. But right now I'm not quite there, and I know it. This day is all I have.

I don't claim to know everything about English, and that's probably the only reason I have survived as a teacher. Because that's precisely what I can delight in about my job: this state of constant discovery. I learn something new every day, from books, from my students, from discussions, from challenges or insights. I savor reading and writing, and that includes reading the work of my students. I have been both an unwaveringly resolute workaholic and a bona fide slacker. I get overwhelmed, overloaded, distracted, or lazy, and sometimes I just can't help it.

Teaching is a marathon, not a sprint. You have to pace yourself. Focus on *your* race, not someone else's, and focus on defining your own "destination," whatever or wherever that may be. To paraphrase an African proverb, "She who wants to run fast will run alone. She who wants to run far will run with others." The best way I've overcome my "will I ever be as good as Tallie Teacher down the hall?" is to focus on seeking out the teachers with whom I *do* connect. The more I dare to reach out, the more teacher friends I make, and the more I spend more time learning from them and laughing with them and trying to be there for them instead of comparing myself to them. We teachers are all in this together, and we all suffer from insecurity and anxiety every now and then; that's why we have to have each other's backs. As one of my favorite poets, Nikki Giovanni, once wrote, "We are better than we think and not quite what we want to be. We are alive to the imaginations and the possibilities."

FAIL TO PLAN; PLAN TO FAIL,
OR …
JUST WAIT AND SEE WHAT HAPPENS

Daniel was a senior and a genius. He came into Creative
Writing class one spring morning with a skip in his step,
cheerfully whistling Tchaikovsky's 1812 Overture. "What are
we going to be working on today?" he asked brightly. I was
completely overwhelmed and was doing well just to have
been at school that day. "Um," I clapped my hands together.
"You're going to have a FREE day! Time to write about
whatever you want. For the whole class period."

He frowned, nodded in an understanding kind of way,
then asked, "No lesson plan?"

I nodded sheepishly. And the class went fine because
they all liked to write, but by the end of the period, they
were growing restless and started itching for
goof-off time. And I didn't feel any less overwhelmed after class
was over. I only felt a little more behind, for some reason.
Planning the day's lesson with *some* kind— any kind, really— of
structure, I've learned, is an absolute necessity. And the more
time I spend on planning, the more effective and enjoyable the

lesson becomes. Believe it or not, planning for the semester or year and creating a syllabus can actually be great fun. It can be creative magic. You are laying down the ground rules; you are plotting out the map. You get to decide—within reason—the direction students will take in their learning adventure. (If the term "learning adventure" sounds cheesy, sorry, but it really is an adventure.)

The first thing I have to remember when planning a syllabus or outline is to stay focused on the designated curriculum. I don't want to go off on strange literary tangents and assign *A Raisin in the Sun* to ninth graders if I know darned well the English teacher next door adores teaching it and is going to have them read it in the eleventh grade. I would be stealing her thunder. No matter what might be said about the benefits and pleasures of reading books a second time for closer analysis, introducing students to a book they've already read is being a killjoy, and it takes the fun out of reading because the students who have read the book already know what's going to happen.

You find this out when half of your ninth graders walk in having already thoroughly read and understood *To Kill a Mockingbird* in the sixth, seventh, or eighth grade. They've been told everything they need to know about Atticus Finch by Mrs. Perfect at Strict Middle School, thank you very much, and she's the one who has been teaching for twenty-five years and knows what she's doing and taught them the Shurley Grammar technique so that they can distinguish between an appositive and an adverb, mind you, so naturally it's only correct for them to assume you have nothing new to teach them about this novel, especially since, after all, they already know all the characters and how it ends, and they already did that "Maycomb Mayhem" activity *last* year, and it was already boring the first time, so how will it be any better the second? And who cares what Boo Radley left in the tree anyway? Needless to say, the whole novel is basically spoiled for the rest of the class. So now that I know how it feels, I don't want to do it to someone else.

The same thing goes for assigning literature that's *way* above their reading level. As I wrote earlier, I made the mistake my first year of teaching ninth graders *Silas Marner* because it was on the suggested list and there were a bunch of shiny, unused *Silas Marner* hardbacks sitting there waiting on my bookshelf. I soon found out why they remained shiny and unused. *Silas Marner* is an archaic period piece with an obscure plot that threw my students into a state of bored frustration. However, that class was a bunch of troupers. Only about 7 percent of the class found the book remotely interesting, and even I had to refer to SparkNotes just to understand exactly who Squire Cass was.

After choosing the grade-appropriate works that you can get really excited about teaching, there are a variety of ways to organize your syllabus. You can do it by theme, genre, rhetorical strategy, or even the seasons. You may want to start with some "anchor" novels, sprinkled with related plays, short stories, and poems, or you may want to focus on only one book or bit of writing at a time. Figure out what works best for you, but try your hardest to stick with it.

Investigate as much as you can about how other teachers teach the text, but try to ignore the pedantic tone of course syllabi you find on the Internet or from veteran teachers who believe they know everything there is to know about everything. It will only intimidate you and make you feel inadequate. As long as you are following the rules and staying within the bounds of the approved curriculum, do what you feel comfortable with. And while I'm at it, let me reiterate: throw out any overwhelming feelings of intimidation or inadequacy that other teachers may inadvertently make you feel. Remember, they were in your place once, too. Remember, be a learner as much as you are a teacher, and do things their way when they ask you to. It's great to be a maverick every now and then, but accept that you have a lot to learn from the experts and that you can't do it all by yourself. Listening to veteran teachers and wanting to do things your own way is a tough balance to achieve, but it's very necessary.

When determining which books, stories, and poems you want your students to read, I have found it best not to take on too much. It's best to spend more time on a smaller number of works and study them in depth than to rush through as many as possible. Choosing which works to read is challenging. This is mainly because you will quickly find that a lot, if not most, of the novels and stories on the suggested/required reading list, contain somewhat disappointing endings, usually involving, at the very least, death or suicide, and at most, adultery, incest, rape, abuse, and an assortment of other controversial and unpleasant plots and themes. Your students will likely alert you to the dismal nature of these works, usually with the profound complaint "Why does everything we read have to be so *depressing*?"

You may ask yourself the same thing. But believe it or not, there is a valid answer. What I try to tell students who get upset when so many of the texts we read have sad endings is this: That's life. Life is suffering. And literature usually functions as a cautionary guide toward thwarting, acknowledging, or dealing with that suffering. It delivers on a variety of premises, from the villainous decisions of *Macbeth*, which prove how ruthless ambition leads to self- destruction, to the lessons of *To Kill a Mockingbird*, which illustrate the devastating effects of collective racism. This is the point of "sad" endings: to expand our knowledge of suffering, thereby increasing our capacity for compassion.

Your course outline allows you to plot a rough road map for the course, which is vital for both teachers and students. It gives you a greater sense of control and direction over your teaching, and it gives students a greater sense of control over their learning. When students are informed ahead of time about what they can expect in a classroom, they feel more confident and prepared. In a course outline you can save instructional time by providing an overview of rules, guidelines, necessary supplies, what works the students can expect to read, and other details. The course outline also gives students a preview of the general time frame of the units. They can get a sense of the amount of rigor and extra homework time outside of class they will need to devote to your course and can plan accordingly. The course outline also gives students, parents, and administrators an idea of what instruction you will use and how you will guide it. It holds you accountable to administrators for your choice of curriculum and ensures that you are adhering to state standards.

A course outline can also serve as a valuable communication tool. Like most teachers, I typically put my tutoring hours, school phone number, email address, and other information on my course outline, and I have the students and their parents sign a contract stating they have read and are aware of the expectations and responsibilities required in my class. And like most teachers, I usually leave a place for the parents to fill in their contact information next to their signature. I then file the signed contracts so that I have all the parent contact information in one place. Course outlines also serve as a support system for principals and teachers. My current principal usually requires teachers to turn in a copy of our course outlines before the semester begins. That way, if there is ever a question from a parent about expectations, curriculum, discipline, or other matters, he can support us and stand behind the particular requirements and guidelines that were presented in our course outline.

If you are in a typical public high school, you will frequently be asked to turn in your lesson plans. Here is the best tip I can give you about lesson plans, or at least it's what works for me. I don't care how old-fashioned you are or how many other teachers turn in handwritten lesson plans. Don't even consider handwriting your lesson plans—even in pencil. This is for your own happiness and sanity.

Your lesson plans, just like all other types of plans, will always, always, *always* be susceptible to some kind of annoying school-related change. This constant state of change can make things either exciting or unbelievably frustrating. You will find that the activities you carefully planned either take too long or are over too quickly; some students will take longer to finish and some will need more time; some classes for which you have the same preparation will go at different paces; there will be assemblies, field trips, college visits, dentist appointments, pep rallies, sicknesses (yours and the students), substitutes, guest speakers, and all kinds of other seemingly conspiratorial attempts to take your class away from you, quietly snickering at you as you lose valuable class time.

You need a way to be equipped for this constant muddle. In my opinion and experience, if you try to deal with handwritten lesson plans, you create an ongoing cycle of erasing, writing, and rewriting that will quickly drive you and your writing hand insane. Also, there is the possible illegibility factor that comes from trying to write quickly. You need a way to be flexible and organized, and the computer allows for this. Even the functions you can find in the simplest of Microsoft Word documents can create the flexibility and organization you need for effective and smooth lesson planning. Here you can quickly change, edit, copy and paste, erase, fill in, switch, and move around all of the components of your lessons, and you are still set. Technology is ever growing on this front; explore and learn a way that works for you.

There are dozens of pedagogical manuals for lesson plan formats, and I don't want to be a proponent of a certain type of format when there are so many that work for different people. But in plain English, here are the basics of a solid lesson plan.

First, don't feel like you have to reinvent the wheel. Observe master teachers in your school to see how they use engaging lessons that grab their students' attention. You don't have to copy everything those teachers do, but use what they do to inspire you. And with so many resources and countless education blogs and websites, there is no need to go it alone.

You can beg, steal, borrow, barter, buy, or, in many cases, just plain freely *take* so many ideas that you can tweak, modify, and adjust to fit your teaching style and students. A sea of resources is out there waiting for you. Some resources will be top-notch; others will be ho-hum. You'll never know until you try them out in your class. So hold your nose, take a deep breath, and dive in—but don't forget to come back up for air!

So how do you start a lesson? First, you're going to need something right at the beginning of each class that your students can be *doing* (not "reading," not "reviewing," not "preparing") immediately upon entering your room. Think of a lesson as a trip you're going to guide your students through to somewhere new, and hopefully, a place that will change them for the better. As soon as everyone is in the "car" of your classroom, they need to strap on their seat belts, so to speak. Think of the warm-up assignment as that safety belt, a way to get them "strapped in" and focused. Every time I've ever neglected to have a warm-up, or thought it wasn't really *that* important, or just let it slide, just for that day, the result was that my students, no matter their age, have been a bit like small children in a car who aren't strapped in, climbing over the backseats, whacking their siblings in the head, spilling their Cheerios and juice boxes all over the place. Okay, so it's not quite *that* bad in the classroom, but it's not too far off. It's just not the situation you want. Usually, a warm-up is going to be an activity that requires pencil and paper, sometimes the laptop. Whether it's a journal entry, a vocabulary sheet, a review crossword puzzle, or a word search, your students need something tangible to do that engages their brains, eyes, and hands as soon as they take their seats. If not, their brains, eyes, and hands will be elsewhere.

While we are talking about what *they're* doing at the beginning of class, let's talk about where I need to be. That place is going to be: Off. My. Rear.

Not on the phone talking to another teacher, not finishing my morning granola bar, not sitting at my desk going over the last minute details of the day's lesson or reading a text message from my mom, not sitting in front of my computer checking email as the students walk in. All of these activities are barriers and distractions that serve to disconnect my from students before I even begin teaching them. Yes, there will be days when we can't help having to take care of last-minute details, but it's good to keep those days limited. You need to be engaged with your students from the moment they set foot in your classroom.

The very best way to begin class on a smooth note is to be standing at the door welcoming students into your space. It shows you've been eagerly awaiting them. You have been expecting and anticipating. You have prepared and invited them to come in. If you are not there to usher them into *your* space, they are invading it, and it becomes *their* territory. They need to know that you want them there. They need to know that you've been waiting for them and that you've put some thought into the time that you will be spending together for the next sixty or ninety minutes. They need to know that you are confident enough to take ownership of your room. They need to see that you have a direction and a set course for the day. You are navigating them into new waters, and they want to be sure they're in capable hands. If you can give them this sense of welcoming confidence, they will oftentimes listen to you more and strive to work harder. They will want to give you their best.

Once your students have completed the opening activity (call it the "opener," "focus activity," "bell-ringer," "warm-up," or whatever you like), it's time to start the lesson. There are a variety of ways to do that, and there are many resources to find out how, so I won't go into them here. However, you may hear some administrators advise you to keep instruction moving at a "rapid pace." As a new teacher, I don't recommend that you follow that suggestion, at least not at first. Think about it. When you first started roller skating and tried to move at a rapid pace, what happened? You probably thought you were a hotshot until your arms went flailing, you lost your footing, and you ended up ungracefully sprawled in the middle of the rink, humiliated, trying not to cry even though you had a skinned knee while Jimmy Stowalski and his posse were snickering at you, having watched the whole fiasco from the concession stand.

You could find yourself in a similar position if you try to go too fast in your classroom in the beginning days of teaching. If you try to fake it with the kids, they'll catch on. So don't go at a rapid pace. This doesn't mean you should move in slow motion or take ten minutes to explain the meaning of the word "surreptitious." Instead, aim for a moderate pace. Stay focused, directed, patient, engaged, and energetic. And just breathe. You'll get there when you get there.

After the students leave, try to take some time to type up a quick reflection of what went well in the lesson or what you'd like to change for next time. Try to write down anything you may have told the class, whether it was "We'll start unit 3 next week," or, "We will peer edit your essays next Thursday. Having a written reminder will be invaluable later when you can't remember what you said to whom.

And what about planning for the days when you're not there? First of all, try your hardest to get a top-notch substitute. Top-notch doesn't mean unreasonably demanding and strict. Top-notch means he or she treats your students with respect and understanding and makes sure the class stays on task while you're out. One useful tool is to create an entire binder for your substitute that includes anything and everything that might be necessary and useful: rosters, seating charts, helpful colleagues and students, emergency procedures, and the like. I know one teacher who even leaves a couple of bucks in an envelope so the sub can go get a snack from the teachers' lounge.

You never know when you're going to have to be out. Even if you are the healthiest person on Earth and never get sick, when you start working in a school, whether it's a public or private one, it does something to your immune system. You *will get sick*, sometimes unexpectedly. Know how to schedule a sub from home. Know your PIN, username, and whatever else you need to know about using your school's sub system. I rarely got sick until I started teaching, and I rarely had to get a sub until I had kids. When you leave your classroom at the end of each day, leave everything as if you will be out the next day. Leave the room in neat condition with your substitute binder on your desk for easy access.

Planning helps you cover your bases and your rear: make the time for it.

DEALING WITH TEENAGERS TODAY: DOES ANYONE *REALLY* KNOW HOW?

In the high school English classes I took, I have a strong memory of being happy pretty much the whole time, even when teachers did a lot of lecture and discussion. I was perfectly happy to sit back, take notes, and soak up what the teacher had to say. English was always my favorite class, and no one around me ever seemed bored. It was exciting to listen to what my classmates thought about a book and to have a chance to contribute my insights. My classmates and I also enjoyed most of the projects our teachers assigned. My ninth-grade teacher gave us a fun author project, and my eleventh-grade teacher made it mandatory for us to write several drafts of a letter to the editor with the intent of getting it published. It was really exciting to see my letter printed in the *Greensboro News & Record*.

Our high school was rigorous, and our English teachers were experienced, knowledgeable, and respected, or at least that's how they appeared to us. They were all female, and none of them was under fifty. They seemed very gentle, wise, patient, collected, laid-back, and confident. We never saw one of them lose their cool, yell, or even seem to get a feather ruffled. They made it look extremely easy, and I thought they hung the moon; in fact, as I explained earlier, they were the ones who made me want to be an English teacher.

When I started teaching, I thought I could do everything—conduct class, facilitate learning, deliver instruction—just as my teachers had. I thought I would walk in, stand at the front of the class, deliver some wisdom, expertly guide students through literature, and occasionally grade a paper or two. I quickly realized that was not the case at all. Teenagers today! Whew!

I discovered the first caricature of me drawn by a student the spring semester of my first year teaching. I immediately thought it meant I had arrived. One of my freshmen drew it. He and I usually had a relatively good rapport. He was your typical jaded fifteen-year-old: still had a little baby fat and a lisp, had an affinity for metal music, and once threw his book bag across the room for no apparent reason.

I was sitting at the overhead projector at the front of the class when I discovered the drawing. My students and I had all been joking around, learning productively, and I thought class was going well. I noticed out of the corner of my eye that the young man was doodling as he was taking notes. However, when he flipped his paper over, I guess he didn't realize that his masterpiece was in my full view.

My first reaction was amusement. At least it was nothing *too* derogatory—mainly just a hastily drawn face with messy hair and the word "NEWLIN" written across with an arrow pointing down to me. Now, previously, a lot of my students had said I reminded them of Miss Honey from the movie *Matilda*, a role played by actress Embeth Davidtz. They assured me it was a compliment, and I took it, albeit the character did seem quite enthusiastic about Keds shoes.

So that was why this new caricature came as a bit of a shock. When did I become the crazed, tyrannical, one-word "Newlin"? What happened to Miss Honey? Was I turning into Mr. Hand from *Fast Times at Ridgemont High*? So to address the situation, all I did was pause in the middle of discussing the vocabulary word "clemency," eye his paper with a slight smile, and give him a "What was that for?" type look. He could read my expression and said aloud, "What?" in his usual defensive stance, then turned over the paper as if noticing his drawing for the first time. His face immediately turned red, he slowly crossed the picture out and ripped up the paper, and then he casually walked across the room and threw it in the trash. He became an enjoyable and amenable student after that day.

A couple of years later, in the computer lab, one of my students found a picture of me on the school's website and embellished my portrait in Photoshop by drawing a variety of black stripes, zigzags, and doodles all across my face. This time I didn't quietly smile. Instead, I quietly ignited and politely informed him that for being off task and not completing the assignment he was going to make a visit to the assistant principal's office.

Halfway escorting him there, I stopped myself. I realized the only reason he had created the drawing was because I hadn't followed through on my part of the bargain as his teacher. He was bored and unmotivated. Like it or not, I indirectly caused his misbehavior.

It has been a rude awakening to discover that not all of my students respond or are even interested in the way that I liked learning when I was their age (which wasn't that long ago, was it? Was it?). I feel that in the classroom, the student has a responsibility and the teacher has a responsibility. The best classroom scenario seems to be one where both teacher and student have high expectations for each other and follow through on meeting those expectations.

A student's misbehavior can reveal insight into a teaching method that isn't working. It is usually said that students are in the classroom to learn, not to be entertained, but I argue that they learn best when they are meaningfully entertained, as well as motivated, pushed, challenged, disciplined, encouraged, and nurtured.

There are many actions that fall under the umbrella of student misbehavior and distractions, and there are just as many possible reasons for that misbehavior. Anything from an overload of extracurricular activities or slight forgetfulness to dysfunction within the home, to a major personality disorder can play a role in a student's misbehavior.

When dealing with misbehavior in the classroom, you will quickly find that it does little good to get defensive, overanalyze or sympathize too much with your students' personal problems, or blame yourself. I know because I've tried these techniques in the classroom with little success. But students still have to meet expectations—yours and those of the school—and you have to hold them to that, no matter what. You set the bar, and they aim to reach it. That's how it works.

When a student doesn't reach that bar, that student isn't going to care unless you let them know ahead of time what *consequence* they'll have to face. What difference does their misbehaving make unless they have to pay for it? Is it a phone call home? Is it lunch detention? Decide, and stick with it. In my earlier days of teaching, when a student didn't meet an expectation, I always found it easier to react emotionally or permissively. But now I have found it significantly more productive and efficient to give the student a reasonable, non-negotiable, and fair consequence for misbehavior. Conversely, it is also vital to give positive reinforcement and intangible rewards for *good* behavior. Every student is different; what works perfectly with one could turn out to be completely terrible and ineffective with another.

If using consequences doesn't work, or when several students are exhibiting bored or distracted behavior to avoid or escape the lesson, that's when you'll have a pretty good idea that you might be doing something wrong. That's also when you need to consider modifying your instruction and mixing things up a bit more. Take another look at your seating arrangement or classroom management methods.

Sometimes you have to just take a deep breath and opt to not make every little thing teenagers say or do into a battle. You have to be more like an orange than an apple. In other words, develop a thicker skin and realize that more will be revealed, even though it might be a little uncomfortable or even downright hurtful right now. You have to realize that, yeah, that hastily drawn caricature you found on the desk could very well be of you . . . and, yeah, that little clique of fifteen-year- old girls *was* probably snickering at some little quirky thing you did, but you know what? Who the heck cares? You are an adult—you have your adult friends, family, and your life outside of school. This job is not everything, and not everyone is going to like you all of the time.

It's likely that you are not going to always be the queen or king in their eyes that you want to be. Sometimes they're going to think it's not cool to like the teacher. After all, in their view, you've got the power; most of them have little or none. Learn how to empower them. Build them up. See what's good in them. Take the littlest thing they do right and make a big deal over it (without being fake or condescending). Be true to them and to yourself.

Even when your students are acting up, they are still listening to you and watching you, believe it or not. Just don't show how badly you want them to listen. Show that you are wow! so into this subject! and oh boy! will they be missing out if they don't pay attention to this amazing stuff! and they'll have little choice but to follow.

Make the material interesting and relevant to their life. Get with it. Get ready. Pump yourself up. Get some guts. Move around the room a lot. As I used to tell my student teacher, don't be afraid to get up in their space. (But not in a creepy, threatening way, of course.) Connect. Don't let them get too comfortable or complacent. Use your passion. Sometimes you will have to trip up and make an idiot out of yourself. You will have to give more compassion than control. You will have to pick your battles and sometimes turn the other cheek—if you want to survive. That's the only way to grow and learn in this profession. If you expect your students to act like the fully formed, reasonable, mature people commonly found in the adult workplace, you are going to be sorely disappointed—because they are *not* adults.

But they are not as innocent as you think they are, either. They know how to manipulate, and they don't always make wise choices. In my classes at any given time, there have been all the labels: the nerds, the potheads, the camo-wearing hunters, the thrice-expelled, the artsy dreamers, the preppy ones, geeky ones, grungy ones, snobby ones, the ones who couldn't care less about anything. I hope they feel like individuals when they leave my class. I hope they feel seen and yes, liked. If you don't like each of them at first, make an effort to *find* something to like in each of them. That's the only thing that will get you through—that and believing your paths crossed for a reason.

Sometimes you'll get a class in which you just have to hold on and make it through until the end of the semester. It isn't you, and it isn't them; it's just the way it is. The chemistry isn't working. I hope that you'll find it in yourself to do the hardest thing in the world and forgive the universe when stressful, unfair classes like that happen to you. They happen to the best of teachers. You *will* make it through, and you will be surprised at how many students you can and will still reach in such classes. The deck may seem stacked against you, but there are often some hidden aces. Hang in there!

YOUR REPUTATION WILL PRECEDE YOU --
BUT YOU DON'T HAVE TO CARE

In a high school the walls have ears and the ceilings have eyes. We all have to exist together. Get used to this idea quickly. Whether you are perceived as an ogre or a pushover, you will have some kind of reputation as a teacher. As kind and patient and wonderful and gracious and Mary Poppins–like as you *think* you appear on the outside, count on everything you say in private or in public to be quickly broadcast over the entire school.

The same thing goes for other teachers. When students are upset with Ms. Lapinsky for giving them an F on their physics lab assignment, they will often come running to you as their confidant. I am unquestionably sure that the same thing happens in other classrooms when students get upset or annoyed with me (over something they shouldn't be upset or annoyed about in the first place, of course! Sheesh!).

You may have great conflict resolution skills, but there is never an ideal strategy in dealing with these "he said/she said" rumors that circulate among students and teachers. Any new teacher may feel insecure and defensive, knowing that his or her reputation precedes them and is out of their control. It's more detrimental than most people realize.

When the school becomes a cauldron of gossip, who is safe from the criticism? Everyone becomes embroiled. Maybe that's just the way it has always been and always will be, but I choose not to participate. Unless I have been directly hurt or insulted by someone's words or actions, I try as much as possible to *stay out of it*.

And it goes both ways. Call me crazy, but I don't think teachers are acting professionally when they are always speaking negatively about other students. I have been guilty of doing so more than once or twice. I'm not proud of it. Students can find out about such remarks, and it only makes them resent teachers more. It just perpetuates the "us vs. them" mentality that leads to disrespect and intolerance on both ends.

I view it as my duty to be empathetic with my students' point of view while at the same time sticking up for my colleagues and reminding students to act with integrity. Having a plain old bad day happens to everyone, and both students and teachers can sometimes forget that. So here's my solution. When I hear students making negative personal comments about other teachers, I immediately cut them off with three sentences:

1. "Hey, that's my colleague."
2. "Please remember that in this classroom we don't disrespect anyone."
3. "Do you really think it's fair to talk about people when they aren't here?"

Now if I have a sincere worry that the student or teacher being talked about is in danger, I determine, is it true? Is it fair? Is it necessary? If so, I will handle it differently by mentioning it to a trusted colleague or an administrator.

(Fortunately, I've rarely had to do that.) But handling potentially hurtful comments in the way I've described makes me feel that I am acting with integrity. I have no time for nor interest in petty gossip, and in fact, no good teacher should. The best advice I have ever heard for teaching and for life is to focus on the solution instead of the problem.

Another thing: you have to have an extra good Jiminy Cricket to build a strong reputation as a good teacher. You have to have a sturdy moral conscience. It can be extremely difficult—especially if you are opinionated and passionate like me—to refrain from openly voicing your personal views in the classroom, whether it's your thoughts on climate change, your favorite presidential candidate, or your preferred brand of paper towels. However, it's absolutely necessary to keep such personal opinions to yourself. Classrooms aren't personal platforms.

Understandably, it can be quite tempting to let your opinions fly any which way. After all, here you are in your very own classroom, and rarely do you have another adult in there with you to hold you accountable for your words and actions. You have been given an astounding amount of power, control, and precious trust—from your administrators, parents, and from the students themselves. This is your classroom, and you have the reins. Whatever you say goes. You're the boss.

So you better watch out.

You can't take advantage of this power. Admittedly, keeping your viewpoints in check is a whole lot easier said than done. Many times your students will be all too happy to egg you on. They will encourage you. They will giddily laugh out loud at your tongue-in-cheek wisecracks, opinions, jokes, mutterings, double entendres, and rolled eyes. But you can't let yourself become the star of your very own *Oprah* show. Use your power and influence wisely. You're creating a space for critical thinkers. Everyone in your classroom has to belong and thrive.

Now, you may be the most conscientious person on the planet, and you may be thinking you would never let loose comments slip out from between your lips. But just wait. You will walk into your classroom one day in the middle of March when everyone at school seems to have a bizarre combination of depression from the desolation of winter and giddiness from the anticipation of spring. Neither you nor the students can stand being there anymore, you're having a bad hair day, you're exhausted and burned out, you didn't finish grading papers the night before, all the technology in the building is down, the lesson you planned has gone awry, and all of your students are unruly, inattentive, and bored. You will be desperate for a way to spark their attention.

So when you do present an issue to discuss or write about in class, offer as many sides of the story as possible. Allow students to synthesize a variety of facts, ideas, human experiences, and viewpoints in order to think for themselves. They are not empty vessels in which we pour our experiential wisdom. For example, when my students are discussing the civil rights movement as it relates to the historical and social context *To Kill a Mockingbird*, I am not about to hold back my outrage about what happened to Emmett Till. I invite students (without commanding or preaching) to consider ways the Emmett Till tragedy can be compared to what has happened when it comes to young black men's lives in recent news today. I let *them* talk about it and listen to each other. As much as possible, I let them do the talking and thinking for themselves.

Whether you know it or not, you are the reluctant role model. A lot of times when you tell people you are a teacher, what do they often say? You guessed it. Don't they often say something along the lines of "Oh, you're a teacher? You must be very *brave*! I couldn't do what you do." Well, those people are exactly right. First and foremost, you have to be brave in order to be successful as a teacher. Most teachers get into teaching because they truly want to be good role models. Many are nurturers, helpers, achievers, and pleasers at heart who truly want to make a difference, and they strive to excel at what they do.

Teaching is first and foremost a selfless caregiving profession, hence one of the most susceptible to burnout. If you're burned out, you might yell so loudly that everyone can hear you down the hall, and colleagues and students will form an impression of you. If you're burned out, you might do some online shopping during class time, and a student sees that and tells others, and people will form an impression of you.

To avoid this burnout and the accompanying downward spiral takes *courage*. As author Parker Palmer explains in *The Courage to Teach*, it really does take courage to be a teacher. It takes courage to step up and do and be the right thing despite the unforeseen traps and all the stress you will experience in this profession. Just remember that you aren't alone. There are people who want to help you and people who want to see the best and bring out the best in you. Seek them out. Whether it's your family and friends, a counselor, a therapist, someone in your church, whoever, do what is necessary to take care of yourself, because no one else really can. When you give care to yourself, that's when you can truly live up to your best potential and give care to others. Picture yourself twenty, thirty, forty years down the road. What do you want your legacy as a teacher to be? Equip yourself with the tools to let your story be a happy one.

Every move, every word, every blind eye, gesture, and comment from you could potentially be witnessed and analyzed, whether you are aware of it or not. That is not an exaggeration. Just when you think the students have zoned out and are not listening to you anymore, and you let a seemingly harmless opinion about gun control out of the bag, that's when you will get that nasty email from a livid parent whose indignation over a perceived or real slight you inflicted upon their child will have to be addressed. You will have to deal with it. The best thing to do is teach defensively. Don't give anyone cause to come after you.

Ninety-nine percent of the time, people are not thinking anything about you. They are busy with their own problems and lives. Still, no matter how busy, distracted, or stressed you are, never forget how much influence you have. Just one harmless word or even facial expression can completely change a student's day (or even their week, month, year), for better or worse. No, we don't have to walk on eggshells all day long, but we have to be conscientious about our words and actions. It's a pretty big responsibility, but that's the way it is. Some people don't think as educators we should carry that responsibility, but who else will?

At some point you and your teaching decisions are going to be judged, criticized, and gossiped about, and you will have zero control over it. And sometimes things happen that have absolutely nothing to do with you. You are powerless over it all. But when you think about it, that's rather liberating. As Eleanor Roosevelt put it, "Do what you feel in your heart to be right, for you'll be criticized anyway. You'll be damned if you do, damned if you don't."

BUILDING AND MAINTAINING APPROPRIATE TEACHER-STUDENT RELATIONSHIPS

Now to the elephant in the book. The previous chapter had "reputation" in the title, so hopefully, you could see this one coming.

I have worked with a handful of teaching colleagues who were forced from their teaching positions because of accusations of improper conduct. One was blatantly guilty of having an affair with a student and faced felony charges; the others were only accused. Proof of misconduct in some of these incidents was never shown one way or the other, but the shroud of hushed whispers, pointed fingers, and ignominy was still haunting. Worse, the children affected were damaged, in one way or another. So, yes, these troublesome situations happen in real life, and they are heartbreaking on all kinds of levels, most of all for the victims.

These days it seems a newscast can't go by without some story of a scandalous "affair" between a teacher and a student. It's not an "affair," however; it's abuse. Sometimes the teacher ends up in jail; sometimes the two get married. However the story ends, it usually gives everyone a sick feeling in the pit of their stomachs.

Inappropriate relationships between teachers and students are often treated as a taboo or "hush- hush" subject when the topic really needs to be confronted and discussed. Instead, when it happens, the principal and school system are questioned for not acting sooner. Infuriated parents now wonder about current teachers, or they lose trust in other teachers. Current students who truly liked the teacher are at first in denial, then shocked, disheartened, and traumatized. They lose faith in adults and role models whom they trusted. So lately it seems the public education system has a disease on its hands for which there is no apparent cure. So what is the next logical step? As the adage goes, an ounce of prevention is worth a pound of cure. So start thinking about prevention. It's pretty simple, actually: don't give *any*one *any* ammunition.

Accept that these types of relationships— however immoral and hurtful they seem—*do* occur. And especially if you are young, new to a school, and no one knows or trusts you yet, your every move will be scrutinized, most times without your knowing it. You need to avoid any hint, any glance, any possible perception of something that should not be there between you and Johnny or you and Jane in the front row. Teach like your hair's on fire, advised one award-winning educator. Before you do that, however, I think it's wise to teach like every student's parent is in the classroom with you.

If you have not done so already, join a teacher's union. After that, my best advice is to treat all students–male and female—as your children, because they *are* children, and each one of them is somebody's baby. They may look like adults, act like adults, even sometimes think like adults—but they are *not* adults. Each of your students is someone's beloved, innocent son or daughter, and don't forget it.

Children are not responsible for overcompensating for emotional or psychological affirmation we didn't receive in the past. We must attain confidence in ourselves today. Self-esteem issues can be hard to deal with, but if you need an adolescent's admiration to boost it, you have a problem. Is there some underlying emotional pain, loneliness, or other unmet need you need to work through? It's okay, as long as you deal with those issues before they deal with you. If you think you are going to be susceptible to something that you know is illegal, talk to someone. Get some help! It's not worth your job, your integrity, and your lifelong reputation, or an indelible mug shot whenever anybody googles you. Snap out of it, and be the adult. Even if you are not biologically old enough to be your students' mother or father, act like you are.

Have a life outside of school! Avoid becoming a workaholic and spending all of your waking time with or for your students, because doing so blurs the boundaries. And you have to think about boundaries! Always leave your classroom door open, and hold no tutoring before or after school without a witness. Use appropriate body language, and wear appropriate attire. You don't always have to necessarily look like Clark Kent or Marian the Librarian, but you should wear professional, mature clothing that suits your personal style as well as your position. Avoid dressing like the students or wearing suggestive or revealing clothing—no matter what any of the other faculty may be wearing. How you carry yourself speaks volumes. No matter your height or size, maintain a strong, commanding physical presence in the classroom and show that it is *your* domain. What you say and do in the classroom follows you—just because you are around teenagers all day doesn't mean you can act like one. You are always *on*, always observed, always scrutinized. And consider the potential of *all* the emails you write— whether on your personal or professional account— to be printed across every billboard along every highway in every state. That may be an exaggeration, but in some ways, it's not.

Understand what personal information is appropriate to share with your students. Examples of appropriate sharing would be that you are training for a marathon, or you have a loved one battling an illness, or a story of how you fell down and got back up during a basketball game when you were their age or a little advice about what to expect at college. Examples of inappropriate sharing would be details about your personal relationships or your personal medical problems, what you texted to your girlfriend in an argument, any type of profanity, how students can connect with you on your personal Instagram or Facebook account, the party you attended last weekend, what you have been smoking, or the nature of your consumption of alcoholic beverages. This type of sharing may make you look "cool" in some students' eyes, but these same students will also see you as unprofessional or immature, and they will feel they no longer have to take you seriously. Once their respect for you is lost, a real decrease in productivity and achievement in your classroom can and often will follow. And that comes back to *your* job. When in doubt, remember that appropriate sharing always includes real-life examples that serve to *enrich and inspire* students, not distract, entertain, or confuse them.

Finally, no offense, but your physical traits won't be here forever. Your kindness, compassion, expertise, patience, and dedication will. Those special qualities of yours are divine gifts that are here to stay, and they will grow if you focus on them. They are yours to give, and they are the best you have to give. Your students deserve that.

SURVIVING THE BUREAUCRACY OF EDUCATION

A few years ago, an anecdote began circulating through the Internet called "The Teaching Prospect" that went something like this:

After being interviewed by the school administration, the eager teaching prospect said, "Let me see if I've got this right."

•   You want me to go into that room with all those kids, and fill their every waking moment with a love for learning.

•   And I'm supposed to instill a sense of pride in their ethnicity, modify their disruptive behavior, observe them for signs of abuse and even censor their t-shirt messages and dress habits.

•   You want me to wage a war on drugs and sexually transmitted diseases, check their backpacks for weapons of mass destruction, and raise their self-esteem.

•   You want me to teach them patriotism, good citizenship, sportsmanship, fair play, how to register to vote, how to balance a checkbook, and how to apply for a job.

•   I am to check their heads for lice, maintain a safe environment, recognize signs of anti-social behavior, offer advice, write letters of recommendation for student employment and scholarships, encourage respect for the cultural diversity of others, and oh, make sure that I give the girls in my class fifty percent of my attention.

• My contract requires me to work on my own time after school, evenings and weekends grading papers.

• Also, I must spend my summer vacation, at my own expense, working toward advance certification and a Master's degree.

• And on my own time you want me to attend committee and faculty meetings, PTA meetings, and participate in staff development training.

• I am to be a paragon of virtue, larger than life, such that my very presence will awe my students into being obedient and respectful of authority.

• You want me to incorporate technology into the learning experience, monitor web sites, and relate personally with each student. That includes deciding who might be potentially dangerous and/or liable to commit a crime in school.

• I am to make sure all students pass the mandatory state exams, even those who don't come to school regularly or complete any of their assignments.

• Plus, I am to make sure that all of the students with disabilities get an equal education regardless of the extent of their mental or physical disability.

• And I am to communicate regularly with the parents by letter, telephone, newsletter and report card.

• All of this I am to do with just a piece of chalk, a computer, a few books, a bulletin board, a big smile AND on a starting salary that qualifies my family for food stamps! You Want Me To Do All Of This And Yet You Expect Me . . . NOT TO PRAY!!

...So I have some news. Of course you can pray, silly. You just can't do it in a way that alienates others. And the above job description is absolutely accurate. That catalog of gripes is, in fact, the precise job of a teacher in a nutshell.

But here's the good news: you don't *have* to adopt the woeful, overwhelmed attitude of that teacher prospect; in fact, you can't. When I first started teaching and overheard the complaints of veteran teachers, I never understood why they felt so burdened. I thought, *just follow the rules, fill out the forms, do what they ask— no big deal.* As much as I possibly can, I still choose to think this way. I refuse to allow myself to become disillusioned and disheartened. If I ever become complacent and lose my enthusiasm for teaching, I will make a gracious exit. In the meantime, I follow the rules to the best of my ability. I admit that I sometimes find it easier to ask for forgiveness instead of permission. As a teacher, you will frequently be asked to do several different things that you may or may not agree with, and few people will actually check up on whether or not you actually did them. So make a good faith effort, but don't get resentful and stressed trying to bend over backward for somebody who is never going to even follow up with you. Learn to say no. Have boundaries. Don't allow yourself to succumb to hubris or murky ethics, but simply view yourself as a professional.

Also, have an escape route. What other jobs and careers can you do? Keep your résumé updated. Be prepared to leave at any time. Not because you necessarily plan to, but because you need to really know your worth and that the bureaucracy does not hold your life's fate in its hands. You are not a workhorse. Value yourself! You are a talented professional with choices, and when you know in your bones that you have chosen to be there, even with all the other options you have, you will be filled with a newfound sense of lightheartedness and even gratitude. Value yourself. Be a teacher because you *want* to be, not because you seemingly have no other choice.

If you want to survive in public education, as a colleague once advised me, you have to learn how to work smarter, not harder. (I'll talk more about this later.) If you try to do every little single little thing you've been told you must do, you will become, like the teacher prospect, daunted, hopeless, and miserable—before you even have a chance to get started. You simply can't complain about every little thing, or you will wind up miserable.

If I can sum up how to survive bureaucracy in one word, that word is "prioritize." Those forms due to administration go at the top of your priority list; searching the web for the world's best lesson plan when teaching chapter 4 of *Wuthering Heights* does not. (Yes, that task *is* on the list, but it's not at the top.)

Attendance is another top priority. You have to take it every single day, and it's a big deal if you don't. (Schools are big on maintaining accurate records. In some school districts, teachers can be subject to disciplinary action for not taking attendance.) You can't be late with grades or deadlines for payroll forms. You can't be absentminded. You *have* to attend meetings. It's just not because they'll look at the sign-in sheet and see you didn't attend. It's because the meeting you miss is inevitably going to have some crucial piece of information that if you miss, will send you up the creek. Communication with parents is also at the top of the priority list. There are a bunch of other priorities. Do your homework, figure out what you absolutely have to do, and let the other stuff fall into place below. But you *can* make it simpler than it seems. Just do your very best.

If you want to survive, you can't create unnecessary battles for yourself.Dealing with the various expectations and demands of administrators, other teachers, parents, and students can often be unpredictable, and unpredictable can be scary. I once had a parent email me, my principal, and the superintendent about a supposed issue in my class that never took place. She accused me of making a remark against her son in class that I never made. Beyond feeling indignant, naturally, I was baffled and saddened for these parents. I hated that they were going through such stress of worrying about their son. When someone doesn't like something you said or did, and you know that they have a point and you should probably apologize, that's one thing. But when someone completely fabricates a falsehood about you and accuses you of being the one who is lying, it's terrifying. It's like living in a dystopian novel. Thankfully, I had a colleague who had been in the classroom during the alleged incident, and she was able to vouch for me in the meeting with the parents.

The first piece of advice from my great aunt Gloria Turlington, a veteran teacher who has given me invaluable teaching guidance over the years, was to join a teacher's union so that if and when you do find yourself in a moment of someone else's temporary bout of insanity, you can have legal representation available to assist you. The dues for such unions aren't cheap, but the peace of mind they provide is priceless.

In the meantime, do your best each day to stay centered and in your own emotional "hula hoop," as it's sometimes referred to. On a typical day, you are interacting with a minimum of approximately seventy to seventy-five brains, each with its own individual agendas, frustrations, joys, concerns, perceptions, ideas, opinions, and emotions. It's important to have a solid center and be secure within yourself. You will encounter a countless variety of feelings and viewpoints from all kinds of people. Therefore, you have to stay grounded and be true to yourself, and try your hardest not to allow anyone's "crisis" to rattle you.

In a bureaucracy or any workplace, really, you can become susceptible to letting someone else's insecurities, issues, or even personality disorder manipulate you without realizing it. You may question what you are doing wrong when it's someone else who has the issue. Especially if you are young, you might be quick to blame yourself. *Don't!* Stand up for yourself and be confident. You say you don't know how to do that? Look the person in the eye and restate why you think what you think, or chose what you chose, or said what you said, or did what you did. Show your backbone (in a polite, calm way). Try your very best not to allow someone else's problem to become your problem. You deserve to be treated with respect at all times, just as everyone does. Stand strong.

THE TESTS ARE ON FIRE (AND YOU DON'T GET AN EXTINGUISHER)

I had a weird dream the other night: it was final exam day, and my third block class reported to the correct classroom to take their exam. I hurried into the room, but then realized I didn't have their exams with me. I rushed all over the school, looking for the exams. Come to find out, the exams had never been delivered to the school by the exam people in Examland. I continued rushing around the school looking for help. The clock was ticking, and I was running out of time. I passed my 4th block students in the hallway, who were bombarding me with questions I couldn't answer: "What room do we go to for our exam? Where are our exams? When will we get to go to lunch?" Finally, I spotted my principal in the hall. "My exams are missing!" I exclaimed to him. I was certain he would do all he could to solve the problem. But all he did was shrug, then said, without making eye contact, "Well, it could be worse. You could have parking lot duty every afternoon." Then he just walked away. (In real life this is pretty uncharacteristic of my principal, so it made it all the more unsettling.) In the dream, I passed teachers in the hallway and kept smiling at them to hide my panic.

"Did you hear about Newlin?" I could hear them whispering to each other. "They never sent her exams."

126

Finally, after scurrying around the school to no avail, I decided there was nothing to do but take my students down the street to the local park and have a picnic.

If you are living in the United States, you may have heard about a wonderful little concept called "No Child Left Behind," which basically means if students don't make at least a 3 on an End-of-Course (EOC) test, they have to retake the course. The highest they can get is a 4. There is even more standardized testing fun now when it comes to certain schools that have added pressure to keep students' scores even higher above standard. They not only have to pass; they also have to do better than they did the year before. This is known as making adequate yearly progress (AYP). Before you get lost in all the acronyms, let me break it down: if the kids don't make AYP with their EOC, you are basically UTC (up the creek).

Although the No Child Left Behind initiative is officially over, standardized tests are still a huge part of the teaching equation. And even if you have an amazing principal who appreciates all of her teachers no matter what, she has probably made clear the pressure riding on you and all academic teachers. If you don't perform wonderfully, those who are attempting to dismantle public education will have "proof" that everyone in public education is goofing off. (Although the truth is that teachers actually do engage in plenty of goofing off—but only at appropriate times, and never during fire drills.)

So the point is that, like it or not, teachers are evaluated based on their students' test scores. Plain and simple. If we jump through a hoop, we get to keep on doing what we've been doing. If we don't jump through the hoop, we will be questioned. It's not fair, but that's the way things are.

One particular class of Honors English 9 I had my second year had driven me, shall we say, a little bit crazy. They were my last class of the day, and the last class of the day for anyone is pretty much when both students and teachers may be somewhat (alright, sometimes *completely*) out of steam. Needless to say, at times this particular class was inattentive, inappropriate, off task, hormonal, lazy, unengaged, and basically downright irritating. They actually led me to raise my voice once or twice, and as a teacher, I've always made it a point never to raise my voice. But the truth is, I always still loved 'em more than my luggage. (In case you haven't heard the expression, it's one of my favorite lines from the movie *Steel Magnolias*.) They always made me laugh, and even at their worst, they were still the best.

So after pounding test prep into their heads even more than usual over the final couple of weeks of school, I made them do one more review game and listen to one more last-minute motivational lecture on relaxing, taking their time, reading carefully, getting plenty of rest, and letting their minds take over during the exam. I told them that of course, they were brilliant geniuses who were probably smarter than the people who make up the test, but that shouldn't trip them up. They should be like the tortoise, not the hare. They should be like the goat, not the jackrabbit. (That's when I started to lose them.) So I told them a little anecdote about my marathon the previous weekend (I had run an arduous and exhausting marathon in San Diego, but I kept going and made it to the finish line), and their eyes got big, and they took in every word I said like the innocent little cuties they are, no matter how grown up they may try to act.

The morning of the exam I brought my students orange juice and blueberry muffins, told those who were goofing off to stop goofing off, wrote "Good luck! You can do it" on the board, said a silent prayer, then left them to their own standardized test–taking devices.

I was on pins and needles all day. In the afternoon, the school counselor, who was usually seen with a coffee mug in his hand and chewing gum in his mouth, and who was a stickler for completing standardized testing as precisely and thoroughly as possible, banged loudly on my classroom door. I thought the building was on fire. When I opened the door, he said, "Hey, superstar," then held up the EOC scores in front of me. My mouth dropped as he gave me a big hug. (He wasn't usually one to give big hugs.) It was straight 4's down the sheet, except for two students who made a 3.

I was beyond proud of my students. They had knocked it out of the park. They had come through for themselves—and for me. But, then, that's what I got for teaching all of these artistic geniuses.
Even when they drove me to the loony bin, they were still the brightest, sweetest, funniest, most talented, wonderful kids in the county, and I felt like the luckiest teacher in the state.

But the bad news is, that was only one battle in a long war. The next semester, I had a class that was the complete opposite. We met in the morning, and they were all eager, acquiescent students who never (hardly ever) made me raise my voice. However, instead of coasting through, this class just barely scooted by on the EOC. In later years at different schools, I had classes who failed their end- of- course exams.

The truth is that as teachers in public schools in America, we are expected to be miracle workers, and if the students don't achieve on standardized tests, it's usually the teacher who is to blame. The powers that be don't just compare teachers' methods; they also constantly compare the test scores of teachers' students as the unquestioned measure of success. When there is a discussion of results, it's almost always termed "Mrs. Y.'s scores" as if Mrs. Y. herself took the test instead of the students. It's almost never "the students' scores."

When students' success or failure is always traced directly and unquestionably back to the teacher, it encourages a culture where children are carried and coddled through without accountability, and many of us teachers think that's not only unfair but dangerous.

What to do? I'm not quite sure. Some experts undoubtedly have some answers; I certainly don't. I do know that standardized tests matter. They do have an impact on your job. As of this writing, there's no way around it. You will be under pressure to get your students to achieve the highest scores. Let it break you or make you stronger; it's your choice. You will be tested as much as your students. It won't be fun. It will be grueling and will take energy and stamina. Do your best each day to prepare them for those all-important tests, but more importantly, prepare them for the test of life. That, as I now see it, is all we can do.

SOMETIMES LET THEM HAVE DESSERT FIRST

My students usually report that they have at least *some* fun in my class. Even when it's the most serious day of the most serious week of the most serious month of the school year, there are still good times to be had. I first learned about making fun part of learning one day, on the seniors' final day of school. At 6:45 AM eight of them showed up for our last-day ceremony. A humble, wise, cool, grandfatherly teacher who taught next door, was every student's favorite and seemed to have his ever-present camera at every event, invited us to join in his senior send-off tradition of reading aloud a sonnet at sunrise, then going out for all-you-can-eat pancakes. So at 6:47 I rolled in (later than my own students, silver travel mug of coffee in hand), and we walked to downtown Greensboro together to a statue of the author O. Henry. After he took the students' pictures, the grandfatherly teacher praised us for being early risers by reading aloud "Composed upon Westminster Bridge," Wordsworth's sonnet that celebrates sunrise in the city:

Earth has not anything to show more fair:
Dull would he be of soul who could pass by
 A slight so touching in its majesty:
This City now doth, like a garment, wear
The beauty of the morning; silent, bare,
Ships, towers, domes, theatres, and temples lie
Open unto the fields, and to the sky;
All bright and glittering in the smokeless air.
Never did sun more beautifully steep
In his first splendour, valley, rock, or hill;
Ne'er saw I, never felt, a calm so deep!
The river glideth at his own sweet will:
Dear God! the very houses seem asleep;
And all that mighty heart is lying still!

Isn't that lovely? Would any of these students remember that exact sonnet later in life? Probably not. Did they have an experience of simple beauty, small triumph, and some type of awakening related to powerful literature, whether they appreciated or will even remember it in years to come? I believe yes. It's crucial to connect students to their communities and empower them. Take them outside to write sometimes. Plan fun field trips and guest speakers; these moments are as much for you as they are for the students. Yes, entertainment can be part of teaching and learning. Let the students help you come up with fun ideas. One year, instead of the typical reading aloud or acting out the trial scene from *To Kill a Mockingbird*, I had a talented class that brought it to life. The drama students were in charge of writing and acting out a script; the vocalists, guitarists, and pianists created an original soundtrack; the dancers choreographed and performed an interpretive dance; the art students designed and published their own "Maycomb Tribune"; and the music production kids created a radio broadcast for the citizens of Maycomb. Each student had an opportunity to shine by contributing his or her own unique gift, and they all had a creative blast in the process. Try doing something simple and spontaneous just for the silliness of it. When my ninth graders were acting out the final scene of *Romeo and Juliet*, I impulsively decided to somewhat loudly play "Time to Say Goodbye" by Andrea Bocelli and "End of the Road" by Boyz II Men. Without missing a beat, my students went right along with it and started lip-syncing and flailing around melodramatically. They were awesome. More recently, when I have my students read O. Henry's short stories, we go to the O. Henry Hotel, where his short story is printed on the upper wall of the lobby. I once took my creative writing class on a field trip to Hanging Rock State Park, and we wrote by the waterfalls. I took another class to the local art museum and we did some exercises with writing and art.

When my ninth graders finish reading *To Kill a Mockingbird*, we go to a local Southern historic courthouse and sit in the jury box and the witness chair to get a feel for what it would have been like to be part of that trial. Then we have "The Okra Show" in the school media center. The students dress up like characters from the book and bring in Southern-style food, such as fried chicken, okra, lima beans, collard greens, biscuits, cornbread, and pecan pie, and are graded on how much they refer to the book and walk, talk, and act like their character. As I mentioned earlier, one year my tenth graders encouraged me to have a cultural celebration for each continent from the world literature we read. After we read *Siddhartha*, we had India Day; after we read *Julius Caesar*, we had Italy Day and went to an Italian restaurant. Such times are really fun (for most of them, at least), and they *are* learning. Involving multiple senses like this can often help students retain what they have learned too.

My students also had the idea to write their own children's books and read them to kindergarten classes at the nearby elementary school. And our school's art teacher (Lisa, the amazing one I mentioned earlier) was right by their side helping them with the materials and with creating, organizing, and binding their books.

Collecting permission slips, arranging for transportation, recruiting chaperones, and turning in receipts and money may seem like a bit of a hassle, but schools are somehow filled with angels everywhere who are more than willing to help you. The temporary hassles are a small price to pay when you see the looks of delight on your students' faces and know that they are young, free, happy, learning something, and, best of all, creating amazing memories that might even help shape their identities.

A few educators may disagree, but I believe that movies and resources like online educational games, helpful hints, reference sites, and online book summaries *do* have their time and place in the English curriculum. In fact, the ever growing amount and variety of digital resources and tools out there can be overwhelming. It's all a far cry from my high school educational experience, when most of my classmates had only just learned of some strange new technological phenomenon called "The Information Superhighway." Today it's called the ubiquitous internet, and I believe it's actually *not* the devil.

When used correctly, technology can and should be our friend in the classroom. I won't yell at my students for doing an internet search to find out more on a chapter from a book if they didn't understand it. I actually feel they should be commended for going the extra mile to further their understanding. The key is that online resources serve as a *supplement*, not a *substitute*, for what the students are reading. That said, if a student plagiarizes, read them the riot act. Contact their home, email the principal, and give that kid a good talking to and a zero with no opportunity to resubmit their work. Better they resent you now than continue the lazy, disastrous (not to mention illegal) habit through their academic career.

As for movies, I'm quite picky about which ones I show in class. If I am going to show any films at all, they must be illuminating, informative, meaningful, and captivating. And those usually include oldies but goodies, whose timelessness is proven in their ability to mesmerize the "Z" generation we teach today who purportedly can't be goaded into focusing on anything besides their smart phones for any sustained period of time. Whenever I show my favorite movie, *Dead Poets Society*, in class, there is nothing better than observing the hypnotized, smiling expression on the kids' faces while they are watching it. It's so much fun to see how much they enjoy it, and I always get something out of the essays they write after viewing the ending of the film in response to the prompt "Would you have stood up on the desk?"

The purpose of showing a movie in class is not to simply fill time. (I mean, what kind of teacher would just pop a video in while she sits behind her desk to relax, grade papers, check email, or plan lessons . . . certainly never me! Gosh!) In all seriousness, you have to follow the correct protocol: make sure you have the copyright license, fill out the form explaining the film's learning objectives and connection to the curriculum, get your principal's approval, and get all of those parental consent forms signed.

In order to discern whether a film fits the bill, my test is whether or not I actually want to come out from grading papers behind my desk and watch the movie with my students or not. If I wouldn't sit through it, I try very hard to not make them sit through it by previewing and choosing suitable films in the first place. For example, when my first class of seniors was studying themes of the hero, the supernatural, courtly love, and chivalry in British literature, the media center's recommendation was a dreadful 1950s Arthurian legend remake with Ava Gardner that only served to bore them to tears. So I opted instead to show them excerpts from the popular 1987 classic *The Princess Bride*. It had all the right elements: medieval setting, the supernatural, sword fighting, a princess in distress, giants, and vengeance, as well as humor to make it more learner- friendly.

My favorite literary work to teach is *Romeo and Juliet*, and I was once in a quandary about what version of the film I should show my freshmen as part of that study. In semesters past, I had tried showing excerpts from the 1968 version of the movie (starring Olivia Wilding and Leonard Whiting, which is excellently crafted but can be outdated, overacted, and melodramatic) and the 1996 Leonardo DiCaprio/Claire Danes version (a personal favorite, but many parts are a bit violent, controversial, or traumatic for the innocent eyes of my freshmen). Another reason for not showing that version appeared one year when a student exclaimed, "OMG. Leonardo DiCaprio is *soooo* cute!"

Another student replied, "Dude, he's so old! He's, like, fifty."

I interrupted: "Ahem! Leonardo DiCaprio is the same age as I am, thank you very much!"

And then laughter erupted.

I eventually came to a far more entertaining, engaging, and creative solution: excerpts from the multiple Academy Award–winning *Shakespeare in Love*, with Gwyneth Paltrow and Joseph Fiennes. Modern enough for them to relate, yet not so fresh out of the theaters that they all would have seen it, the film is a behind-the-scenes/could-have-happened tale of how "Will" may have come to write (as well as perform in) his legendary play about the ill-fated, star-cross'd Romeo Montague and Juliet Capulet. With a stellar cast, impeccable direction, magical acting, and a witty storyline, the movie is a dream. It also includes relevant historical and literary tidbits to further enlighten my precious ones. They got a huge kick out of seeing the fictional Shakespeare's inspiration unfold, and they amazed even themselves with the insightful connections they were able to make between the plot of Shakespeare's life and works and the historical events as portrayed in the film. The movie is not without its PG-13-rated scenes, but those can be bypassed quickly with a prudent click of the fast-forward button on the remote control. Whenever I show choice clips from *Shakespeare in Love*, laughter abounds, a few tears are shed, and every now and then at the end of the movie, I sometimes think I hear a collective classroom sigh.

Keep your eyes open for movies that connect to literature in thought-provoking ways, especially those that will keep your students engaged and stretch them mentally and emotionally. For example, I like to show excerpts from the *Fried Green Tomatoes* (1992) and compare the motifs and characters with *To Kill a Mockingbird*. When a whole class is experiencing a film and trying to hold back sobs together, it's unforgettable. I also like to show the closing argument in the trial scene from *A Time to Kill* and have my students compare it to Atticus Finch's closing argument in *To Kill a Mockingbird*. What did the character Carl Lee Hailey in the first film say that Tom Robinson in the second didn't, and why? For the book *Siddhartha* by Herman Hesse, we view excerpts from the 2016 film *Lion* to compare many themes, including the characters' internal conflicts and quests for identity. The possibilities are endless.

Regardless of which films you choose to supplement your teaching, always make sure you have some type of study guide or written assignment to accompany them in order to hold your students accountable for paying attention and learning.

Whether it's a field trip, a movie, or something else fun, none of the activities will work without one crucial element: your active, engaged presence. You're their teacher, not their babysitter. Monitor them closely each step of the way; make sure they're paying attention; ask higher level questions of them, check for understanding, and continually tie it back to what they are supposed to be learning. After all, if you're going to let them eat dessert first, make sure the treats you give have been prepared with care and enough time to be savored. Bon appétit!

WHEN THE GOING GETS TOUGH…
YOU KNOW THE REST

This is the hardest lesson I have had to learn as a teacher: if I want to fully succeed and fully do my job, I must be tough.

Now, let me define what "tough" means. As I mentioned earlier, it doesn't mean yelling, belittling, or insulting. It doesn't mean being hardened or heartless. It doesn't mean you never smile. Tough doesn't mean having to be a witch with a capital B.

Tough means steely. It means strong: tougher than the apathy or moodiness of a teenager, tougher than crisis mode management, tougher than failed experimental education programs, tougher than an irate parent's email or phone call, tougher than your guilty conscience scolding you for the papers left ungraded.

You have to be tough in order to survive. To be tough, you must humble yourself. You must roll with the punches. You must think positively. If you pray, pray. In the words of MC Hammer, "You've got to pray just to make it today." He is exactly right.

I am a huge fan of the movie *Steel Magnolias*; in my senior year of high school, I even had the role of M'Lynn in the play. The Steel Magnolia is an example of toughness. She (or he) is the kind of person many of us know and admire. Here's how I described the female version of the Steel Magnolia in an article for the website *Yes! Weekly* in May 2005: "Just like the characters in the movie, the Steel Magnolia displays strength, [internal] beauty, and ingenuity instead of fear, dishonesty, and guilt. She handles stress of all levels with wit, courage, and, most of all, friends. She is real; she doesn't conceal. The Steel Magnolia is found in our mothers, grandmothers, sisters, aunts, and friends, and it is what we strive for most in ourselves." A Steel Magnolia is what I hope to be as a teacher.

Most times when we think back to our favorite English teachers, we think about how easy they made it seem. Maybe it was their creativity or their caring and nurturing personality. They were very welcoming, kind, and affirming, yet fair. It seemed like they had everything together so seamlessly and effortlessly.

That is exactly the kind of teacher I strive to be, mainly because it's what I responded to as a student. According to Goethe, "Treat a man as he is, he will remain so. Treat a man the way he can be, and he will become that." Those words have been my mantra as a teacher. When someone sees the best in me, is truly interested in helping all students, and makes me feel like I am doing a good job, it pushes me to continue rising to that level and to try even harder to do my personal best.

However, you will find that without rigor and toughness, this caring, overly patient, idealistic method won't work with high school students, especially if they would rather eat a whole jar of spiced artichoke hearts than sit in English class. (And, trust me, some of them really, really would choose the artichoke hearts.)

Some days you won't want to be tough. You will wonder what the heck is up with your inexplicable feelings of apathy and depression. You will be exhausted. You will be too tired to even explain why you are tired. You will want an escape. You will count down the days and sometimes the hours until summer vacation or another break. You won't even have the energy for anger. You'll say "screw it." You won't feel like going to faculty meetings or holding tutoring sessions, and you may choose to shirk your duties, even though you know that decision will come back to bite you. You will have to be social and put on a smile, even though you know you just can't do it right then. But you will just have to face the world and, much tougher yet, your students. You will have to be tough.

My students had always consistently achieved very high scores on their EOC and AP exams. I believed it was not only because of their inherent intelligence and willingness to work hard but also because they felt valued, accepted, and free to express themselves in my class. This is what made them listen, learn, and strive for their best. As I mentioned in the previous chapters, I also frequently gave them rewards, such as field trips, guest speakers, meaningful and engaging movies, or having class outside.

An affirming, gentle, nurturing yet firm style built positive, open relationships with my students and was what really motivated them, I thought. The bonus for me was that it's how I was able to handle my job as a teacher instead of feeling like I was going to war every day, stressed and burned out. I had to bend sometimes so that I wouldn't break. I didn't make everything a battle.

However, somewhere around my third year of teaching, I began to feel conflicted about my teaching style. It was some of the toughest stress I have ever been through; I even lost sleep over it. It began when my principal, administrators, members of my department, some of my students, and even my mentor started admonishing me to be more rigorous and more of a "taskmaster." The word on the street (or the campus) was "Ms. Newlin is so nice," but to them, nice didn't cut it anymore. Letting the students express themselves didn't cut it anymore. I wasn't doing enough to make the students grow. I felt broken, resentful, and misunderstood. Most of all, I was hurt, because I knew my critics were ultimately right. I'd had it only half right.

Being nice and caring is only one piece of the puzzle of teaching. We can be the most caring teachers in the world, but that's just one of the standards we have to meet. If we can't manage our classrooms or instructional time and are rated "below standard," we ultimately no longer get to teach. Over time I've had to learn how to get tougher. I've had to set higher expectations and push my students to do more and be more. I have to call them out when they're not giving their best, and that's rarely a comfortable thing to do for them or for me. It hasn't an overnight process, and it's something I continue to struggle with at times. Being tough requires a balance between expecting a lot of yourself and giving yourself a break—and doing the same for your students.

I'm convinced that in order to be and stay tough, we teachers first have to be sane. A lot of times when you are stressed to the breaking point, it's probably not going to be a good idea to "tough it out" and deal with teenagers at that moment. Somebody is going to end up in tears. So you can consider implementing something called a "go-away day." (Try not to call it that in front of the students.) My version of a go-away day is to list four or five choices of independent catch-up work my students can do, such as reading, completing study guides, or vocabulary work. I also occasionally let them listen to their iPods (using headphones or earbuds), as long as they are quiet, self-directed, and on task. While they are doing this, I monitor them while catching up on grading papers or filing paperwork. I'm not up there doing my dog and pony show because I simply can't do that every day. For my own mental health and to avoid

142

burnout, once in a while I have to give my students and myself a day to recuperate and simply breathe.

You can be the teacher you naturally are while still being effective. Find that balance. Be honest with yourself. But don't cave into the pressure to try to be something you are not. Embrace who you truly are. For example, if you don't like it when students do things that are disruptive, such as talking when you're talking, texting, putting their head on their desk, or coming in late, address the problem right away. Let their parents in on it. Give the students consequences. It doesn't make you mean or strict or unfair. It demonstrates that you have a backbone. You can do it in a nice way, but you have to do it. You deserve respect. You have an important job to do and don't have time to put up with shenanigans.

Another part of being tough, paradoxically, is being positive and displaying a positive attitude. Even if you may be perceived as the friendly golden retriever of the school, who frequently smiles and tries to be happy no matter what, you have to keep plugging away. That is what will get you through, and it's what will get the students through. A positive attitude is perceived by some as a mindless, cheerful disposition, but it's not. A positive attitude is a *choice*, and it takes hard work and internal strength.

You can get tough by choosing to have a positive attitude about attending mandatory workshops, seminars, and conferences. You can take notes and try to learn something from such meetings. A popular quote goes "If you can't get out of it, get into it." I know, that's easier said than done when it's 5:15 PM in the middle of January, the holiday joy is over, you are hungry, tired, and the meeting is running later than it should because that certain somebody won't quit asking inane questions that don't pertain to anyone else.

Tough doesn't mean crotchety and mean. A few teachers who are burned out seem to have been resolved to be unhappy. Try not to let their choice influence you. Focus on the winners. Focus on those who have what you want, in whatever way that is. Think tender and tough: it's (almost) always enough.

HAVE A LIFE
– AND AN IDENTITY –
OUTSIDE OF SCHOOL

Here is the secret to keeping up your stamina as a teacher: wolf down two candy bars and two cups of coffee every hour on the hour.

What? That doesn't sound like a good idea to you? Okay, then go to Plan B: don't make teaching your entire life.

Taking care of yourself and being happy is one of the best things you can do not only for yourself but also, more importantly, for your students. Managing a classroom of some 28 students—and that's considered a small class size—is one of the most stressful jobs a person can have.

When you perceive yourself only as a "teacher," you risk becoming frustrated, resentful, and moody. At least that's what happens to me every time I start putting self-care on the back burner. The truth is that while teaching is immensely rewarding, the payback simply doesn't happen every day. As a new teacher, you are figuring out your way, and it can be *unbelievably* taxing, exhausting, and time- consuming. You have a universe of pressure and responsibility on you, and the truth is that not every single one of your students and fellow staff members are smitten with you. This job takes more than competence, and it takes more than politeness. It takes everything you've got.

When you make time to relax and develop solid friendships, healthy hobbies and interests, and a social life outside of the classroom, energy begets energy. My first year, I made the mistake of thinking that if I wasn't 100 percent dedicated and focused on teaching 24/7, I would fall behind. What happened instead was that I quickly burned out. I would come in nearly every single weekend and spend hours organizing my new classroom, poring through the file cabinets and all the books, and then plan and plan and plan, obsessively. I didn't realize the toll it could and would take on my mental health.

In the spring of that year, I entered what I can only call a euphoric cyclone. "Euphoric" because it was, well, fun, and "cyclone" because it was dangerous. I stayed out too late and partied too hard to get rid of stress. Thankfully, this period lasted only a few months and didn't lead to any indelible consequences. I think my dumb choices could be attributed to being in my twenties (what a fun and confusing decade!) But the real problem was that instead of dealing with my emotions, I had stuffed down how I really felt about life experiences that I had not even acknowledged as being traumatic: my parents' painful departure from their family business, my own job layoff from the publishing company, the end of a relationship I had treasured, my mother's battle for her life with lymphoma (which, fortunately, she won), even the loss of our beloved family golden retrievers.

My true self and true happiness returned only when I came back to my faith, friends, and family. I also connected that summer with a group of young, new, fun teachers that I could relate to who made me laugh and got me reconnected to my passion for teaching.

So you think I would learn my lesson, right?

Wrong. A couple of years later, I did it again (but without quite as much partying). Again, I became a glutton for volunteering to take on more than I could handle.

My third year of teaching, I decided to try to be a Wonder Woman. I had initially tried to convince my principal to let me teach two different AP English courses, but she was smarter than me and my reckless overzealousness and said no. So I settled for taking on teaching just one brand-new AP course, but I added helping our school guidance counselor co-lead a new service club, helping co- chair the student council, and co-chairing the school's United Way campaign.

Guess what. I failed at all three of the extra tasks. It all came to a head when, ironically, I missed an important meeting about licensure requirements that truly could have been a matter of getting rehired or not. That's when my principal told me she was taking the extracurriculars off my plate and encouraged me to go see a counselor to address my internal conflicts. She said, "If you had a broken leg, would we be sitting here questioning whether you needed to go see a doctor?"

I had become so wrapped up in doing and doing and going and going that I had nearly lost the very thing I was doing and going for.

"A jack-of-all-trades is a master of none" may be a catchy adage, but it's true. You don't have to be Wonder Woman or Superman when you teach. You don't have to continually go above and beyond to earn approval and respect and acceptance. Rarely is anyone going to care. And no one is going to engrave your tombstone with the words "Here lies Jane. She got all her papers graded on time."

I used to take it home with me every day. I prided myself on lugging my purse, lunch cooler (yes, it was not a lunchbox but a sizable portable cooler; we teachers can get as hungry as football players), my portable file folder holder with all the students' quizzes, classwork, and essays in it in different tabbed files, and my black briefcase with my teacher's edition textbook, a huge binder I had compiled with dozens of activities and lessons related to the novel we were reading, copies of any novels we were reading that I wanted to annotate and discuss in class the following day, my humongous calculator I would use to calculate grades, highlighters, pencils, and a variety of blue pens. Admittedly, in those first years of teaching, you will have to bring it home with you because there is simply so much to navigate and comprehend. But when I look back, I could have done just as acceptable a job if I had not made teaching consume my life quite so much.

So this is what I urge you: as much as possible, *don't take it home with you!* Yes, that's right. That's my advice. And it's only because I now have a spouse I adore, two small children who are the center of my universe, two cats (and probably a dog someday soon), and an entire household and busy family life to manage, not to mention other interests, friends, and volunteer commitments I feel passionate about. There was a time when I took work home every night and every weekend. Then I got married. Then I had kids. I still *wanted* to take it home and just couldn't. But now I just admit the truth: I don't *want* to take it home anymore, and actually, nine days out of ten, I just *won't*.

Some teachers are willing to dedicate endless hours outside of school and not get paid for it. That is their choice, and it is an honorable one. Craving more life balance and not settling for less has been a journey for me. Saying no means I'm saying yes to something else. When I say no to grading papers at home, I'm saying yes to getting on the floor and helping my four-year-old with a puzzle. I used to stand at the copier for nearly my entire planning period. A veteran teaching colleague, who typically bounced around in jeans and Reeboks and danced to some imaginary music playing in her head, always seemed light-hearted, cheerful, and on her game. As I stood at that copier every afternoon, she would shake her head and remind me, "I'm telling you, Ms. Newlin, work *smarter*, not harder, work *smarter*, not harder. One day when you have kids, you won't have a choice."

Yes, I just broke one of the cardinal rules of teaching, I know. We're supposed to be martyrs. But think about it: In what other profession do people take work home with them and not get paid for working overtime? Does your doctor take your medical chart home and spend a few hours commenting and giving you feedback on how you can improve your eating and exercise habits? Does your plumber lug your toilet, sink, and bathtub home with her to see if she can fiddle with everything after she finishes dinner? When you eat at a restaurant, does the kitchen staff take your dirty dishes home with them, wash them, and return them the next day?

No. Of course not. In most workplaces, the job is done and the professional leaves. If the job is not done, then sometimes the professional has to come to a stopping point and come back to finish the job the next day. Why should it be different with us teachers? And don't even get me started on using our own money to pay for the necessary materials and supplies needed to do our jobs. In what other profession? Really. (Yes, I know darn well you'll continue to use your own money to pay for supplies, and so will I, but still. We really shouldn't. Maybe someday we won't have to. We can dream, right?)

In all seriousness, why do we teachers feel the need to burn ourselves out with self-sacrifice? If we want to recruit and retain new, talented teachers, why do we perpetuate the idea that they will have to be miserably tethered to their jobs like indentured servants?

Even if you aren't married with kids, finding a balance and other ways to feed your soul will help make you a better teacher. Having a life outside of work is not overrated. Where is your balance? Try to remember who you are outside of your role as a teacher. Are you a writer? A runner? A gardener? A beekeeper, woodworker? A cook? And speaking of cooking, do you feed your *body* regularly with hearty, nutritious food? Do you get exercise to get the toxins and stress out? If you want to thrive, you have to take care of yourself; it's non-negotiable.

One last thing: when I am having *that moment* in the classroom—the moment when I'm feeling frustrated, resentful, and about to just friggin' lose it, I try to remember to picture my "cheerleaders" in the back of the room who are smiling at me, the ones who are more important than this job. I remember, "Oh yeah, that's right. I am somebody's mommy, spouse, daughter, granddaughter, friend, and loved one—not just Ms. Newlin. I have a *life*."

TEACHERS CAN MAKE A DIFFERENCE...
AND A DECENT LIVING

"In all honesty, I just don't know how anyone who has any self-respect can still stay in teaching."

"Those who can do, and those who can't . . .teach."
"Just a teacher? But you could be so much more!"

We've all heard comments like these in one form or another. They can be very persuasive, especially at the end of a long week when you see your former student in the hallway—the one you spent so many extra hours with: building up her self- esteem, grading her essays, planning lessons specifically tailored to her learning style. Then that same student just walks right past you in the hallway with no eye contact or greeting, as if you're invisible. The special bond you thought you had, the sacrifices you made, not to mention the field trips you planned. *Do I even matter?* you might think. *Is this even worth it?* At least that's what I've thought at more than one point. And I'm definitely not the only one who has had such thoughts.

There was a time when I thought seriously about leaving teaching. I met a friend for dinner one night. I had invited her out to discuss how she had left teaching two years earlier and how I might forge a path to do the same. "Get more active on LinkedIn, update your résumé, stay decisive," she advised in a warm, kind, understanding way. When dinner concluded, she added, "By the way, I won't judge you if you decide you don't want to leave teaching."

There had been no dramatic turn of events that led to this new decision to leave. The school year was going fine—it was not terrible, not wonderful. I had simply started to itch for more.

Money, to be exact.

There were so many things I wanted to give or continue giving my kids—a bilingual Montessori education, ballet lessons, soccer; trips to Colorado, Switzerland, and Curacao, to name a few; and, yes, I admit it, cute clothes (for them and for me). I started becoming enthralled with the idea that I could be "so much more" than a teacher. Twelve years into this, was it worth it? And really was I even good at it? I asked my friend at dinner if leaving had been worth it. She admitted that she cried for the first two weeks after leaving, but then she was over it. And she could honestly say that she was definitely happier. She told me her new salary, and it sounded significantly higher than mine. Plus, she got to go to the bathroom, to the break room, or out to lunch whenever she wanted. She didn't have to take work home in the evenings or on weekends. Sure, she missed the long summer breaks, winter breaks, and spring breaks, but twenty thousand dollars extra per year meant a lot of her financial stresses were gone. My eyes glazed over with dollar signs as I heard her talking.

I called my sister to tell her how excited I was about making this new decision to advance my career, to have self-respect about my salary, and to make a better life for my *own* kids for once instead of somebody else's kids.

However, my sister didn't sound convinced. "I just think you should really listen to your heart before moving forward," she gently suggested. She reminded me about the sweet, seemingly endless wonder of having summers with my kids, not to mention two whole weeks with them during the holidays and a full week in the spring. She reminded me that I could leave earlier in the afternoons to pick them up from school and be home before rush hour. As a young mother herself who worked remotely from home, she had a pretty sweet deal, I had thought. Yet she said to me, "I'd give *anything* to be in your shoes. Plus, you were just telling me a few months ago how great teaching was and how much you loved it."

My sister is right a lot of the time. So I thought about what she said. I teach in North Carolina, which at the time of this writing, is notoriously and consistently ranked as one of the worst states in the country to teach. Teacher safety, student-to-teacher ratio, and low teacher income have been just a few of the factors included in this estimation.

But then I did the numbers. Not for the general teaching population across my entire state, or even country. Just for me:

28: the number of students in my largest class that semester

90: the number of minutes in my planning period

60: the number of minutes in my lunch period (which did, some days, include duty, meetings, and tutoring, but they were bearable and even pleasant when I had the right attitude)

8: the number of hours per day I was expected and required to actually be at school

So when it really came down to it, I somewhat had it made. But the most important number was this one: 180. This was the number of days in an official school year, or the number of days I had to be "on" in the classroom doing my job. It also happened to be the number of days when I experienced real joy. That was the one inconvenient piece of my whole plan to leave teaching. It's what I've hopefully illuminated in the previous chapters of this book: the great, deep joy that I experience as a teacher every single day, in some form or another.

It's the sense of kinship and energy I feel when I walk down the hall and hear and see my colleagues working so hard. And there is just something incomparable about working with young people. You never know what they are going to say next. They rarely have an agenda. Sure, you've got your knuckleheads, but most of them are pure-hearted, 99% of the time. You get to see those wonderful looks in their eyes when they "get it." And there is something really special about working with friendly, fulfilled colleagues who respect you and are in it with you, who show you how it's done and are there when you need help. Furthermore, when I subtracted a few teacher workdays and other days for training or staff development, then added a few personal days or sick days that I could take at my discretion, it left approximately a full half of the rest of the year, which meant that 50 percent of the days in a year belong to me to do with as I please: days I can spend fulfilling my own interests, pursuing my own passions, running around with my kids, not having to miss their growing up.

Look, I get it. Teachers should absolutely make more money, and we should work together to make our voices heard on that issue. I realize everyone's financial and familial situation is different, and I realize every school and district is different. I can't argue that. What I do argue is that although the *quantity* of money teachers make should definitely be increased, the *quality* of a life we can potentially enjoy should also be factored into the kind of living that we teachers can make. In spite of the fact that I work in a state that struggles, my school is fairly well- resourced, and I know firsthand that it's not the only school in the state or the country that's doing okay. Many schools actually treat their teachers well. Many people in public education *do* care. Hold out for a good school in which you can teach. Find that school that's right for you, where you will be best and happiest-- because it's out there. Know yourself. You do have a choice about where to teach. If you aren't feeling joy at your current school or you're getting treated like crap, look elsewhere. You're worth it.

Someday my feelings about teaching may change. Leadership may change. My rosters and class sizes and patience threshold may change. I haven't seen it all, and I don't know it all. All I know is that being an English teacher is where I feel I belong today, and today, that's good enough for me.

WHAT IF I TOLD YOU I AM A TEACHER?

What if I told you I am a teacher?

What if I told you that I still choose to be a teacher in a place and age where gun violence has somehow become an accepted norm?

What if I told you that I'd rather spend time planning lessons, grading papers and teaching children instead of worrying about how to keep them alive during lockdowns?

What if I told you that I'm tired of being angry?

What if I told you that I'm tired of being told that my anger is political?

What if I told you that, like millions of educators, I'd get in front of a bullet for my students, but that doesn't mean I want to carry a gun in my classroom?

What if I told you that I have two babies of my own, but the children I teach are all my babies, too?

What if we didn't have to be sad, scared and heartbroken?

What if we said something? What if we did something?

What if we finally stopped the madness?

A LETTER TO YOU

Dear excited, eager, thrilled, frightened, frustrated hopeful, new teacher,

First of all, I really wish that I could give you a big hug. (What can I say? I'm a hugger.) Because I know exactly how you feel. No, it's not a hug of pity; it's a hug of congratulations! Because I know what an adventure lies in store for you. I also know that there are going to be days when you get really, really disheartened, and you'll feel ready to give up. Please don't!

When I came into teaching, I had a hundred different idealistic notions of how I was going to make a huge difference and inspire the next generation. And in many ways, I know that I did have that kind of effect! But in other ways, I look back on those early years of teaching, or even last week's teaching, and believe there were many times when I failed miserably. There's not a whole lot that I can do to change it. I messed up. So what? It won't be the last time. I learned from it, chalked it up to not knowing better, and moved on to the next moment. But I think I would have been an even bigger failure if I had not learned how to do one very important thing: to not take this job (or myself) so seriously. (I can be the most oversensitive, take- things-seriously person in the world, so this was a big challenge.)

Remember that if you even considered going into teaching, there is pretty much an automatically high chance that you have the passion, the intelligence, and, most of all, a heart that's in the right place to do so.

I am also going to give it to you tough. As a teacher, whether you want it or not, you will be the center of attention at least some portion of the time. That's not the tough part, because you already knew that. Here's the tough part: I would be willing to bet that there's a strong chance that you are simultaneously one of the most and least self- centered people on Earth. I apologize for having just completely halfway insulted you. But, come on, you have to admit it: some part of you, however small or large, is in this for your ego. You get to talk about what you want to all day. You get to call a lot of the shots. A lot of this job is about you. Your influence can make or break the day for some kids. And that's okay. The bad news is that whenever I have operated from a place of Ego, I have either flailed or failed, or sometimes both. The good news is that teaching shows me—no, forces me—to transcend that ego. And that's a gift. When it happens, it helps us become more authentic human beings. It's a bit like how the Skin Horse describes the concept of becoming "Real" in *The Velveteen Rabbit:*

"Real isn't how you are made. . . .. It's a thing that happens to you. When a child loves you for a long, long time . . . then you become Real. . . . When you are Real you don't mind being hurt. . . . It doesn't happen all at once. You become. It takes a long time. That's why it doesn't happen often to people who break easily, or have sharp edges, or who have to be carefully kept. Generally, by the time you are Real, most of your hair has been loved off, and your eyes drop out and you get loose in the joints and very shabby. But these things don't matter at all, because once you are Real you can't be ugly, except to people who don't understand."

I won't lie. This process of becoming a real teacher *hurts.* You're going to be hurt, humbled and, at times, even humiliated, with a sense of being tossed aside just like that little threadbare bunny. You don't get paid enough to endure that irate parent phone call, you'll think, and you shouldn't have to worry about that student who cusses at you and threatens to "kick the baby out of your belly" (yes, that happened to me, but what that student didn't know was that my baby would have kicked back). You have so many other priorities besides that seemingly meaningless paperwork, you'll think. There will be days that are so bad you'll seriously consider quitting. EFF. THIS. NOISE, you'll think. But on behalf of the children and nation who need you, I am asking you not to. Because you will get through it. And you will experience great, deep joy again.

Sometimes you may wonder if you're simply at a school that is not where you are meant to be at that particular time. But please don't give up teaching altogether. You care enough to read this book, which means you care enough to let teaching hurt. Every time your heart breaks, it grows bigger, or so the saying goes. You've got it in you. It's in your blood.

As I mentioned at the beginning of the book, when I was first hired as a teacher, my principal took a huge chance, since I was relatively inexperienced and carried that big fat stigma of "lateral entry" (read, "questionably qualified") all over me. But she said she picked me out of several other candidates because she sensed my passion. She told me to be excited about having found my calling and not to apologize for being a lateral entry teacher. She also said, "You can show somebody how to be a good teacher, but you can't show them how to be a good person."

If they don't learn anything else in your classroom, your students will have learned a little more about how to be a better person. That's what matters in the end. You will at times feel discouraged, stressed, or unappreciated, but when you do, it's important to remember the honor that you have, the exquisite responsibility of teaching and preparing adolescents to be communicators, analyzers, writers, and listeners. You have the power to make them feel stronger and better. It's up to you to use this power. When you start to feel down, look for that student who needs you. She might come to see you at lunch. He might need merely a kind word when you greet him at the door. They all might just need a "Hey, how's everybody doin' today?" at the start of class on a rainy winter morning.

As you embark on this journey, I wish you newfound courage and strength and an ability to avoid putting too much pressure on yourself. You are wonderful, and simply by caring you are doing a heck of a lot better than many. So keep on keeping on, and don't give up. I leave you with one more captured firefly. On the first day of school one year, I received an email from a student who had graduated eighth grade and moved on to his first year of high school: "Hey Ms. Newlin just so you know I did get lost trying to find advisory class room, but I did what you said about smiling and I made a new friend."

Did that make you smile and light you up just a little? There's so much more to come. You have the passion. Now go help capture some fireflies.

A LETTER TO BETSY DEVOS, CURRENT U.S. SECRETARY OF EDUCATION

February 2017

Dear Secretary DeVos:

Salutations, as Charlotte from *Charlotte's Web* would say. Did you like that book? It's a good one.

You seem like a very charming and well-meaning lady. If I met you in person, I'd shake your hand and try to use good manners and make you feel welcome in my school and classroom. You are a controversial person in the news these days, however, and I know it must not be easy being in your shoes.

Atticus Finch, also a bit controversial for various reasons, is a character I'll continue to revere because of his lesson to his six-year-old daughter: "You never understand a person until you consider things from his point of view . . . until you climb inside his skin and walk around in it."

So I'd like to ask, with all due courtesy and respect, do you think you might take a moment to consider *my* point of view as a high school English teacher who has taught for thirteen years in North Carolina Public Schools?

Now, just like Charlotte had a job to do, and Wilbur had a job to do, and Fern had the fair and the Ferris wheel and the cows to milk and whatnot, you have a job, and I have a job. And since we're both in education, our jobs are not supposed to be at cross-purposes. Right?

Well, I am currently not convinced that we really have the same interests at heart, and therefore, I am concerned.

It's 9:40 PM and I'm just now finishing all the work I had to do to prepare to be away from school tomorrow for another day. My son was sick with an ear infection last week, and now I'm sick with strep throat, and it's kicking my rear. So, alas, I have to take another sick day.

After I finally completed all of the prep work to be out tomorrow, I thought, *Man, I wish I could tell our secretary of education about this so that she could see just how much work goes into being a teacher.*

And I'm just one of the proficient ones. I'm not extraordinary or distinguished. I'm just, like, makin' it.
Then I thought, *Maybe I will. I will tell all this to Secretary DeVos.*

So here it is: preparing for classes I won't even be teaching tomorrow took me about two and a half hours, although admittedly about thirty minutes of those were spent reading bedtime stories to my three- year-old about all of her various strong female characters. Have you read any of these? There are so many. You've got your socially strong, like, say, Madeline; or imaginatively and emotionally strong, like Doc McStuffins; or physically strong, like Pippi Longstocking; and then the more subtly strong, like Minnie Mouse, who is entrepreneurially strong with that Bowtique she's got going on; and scientifically strong, like Ada Twist; and persevering strong, like Talullah and her tutu.

But I digress. The point is, I have a daughter, and raising her to be a strong woman is hugely important to me, to her whole family. Do you have daughters? Do you let them near your boss? (Because I wouldn't. That's just me, though.)

Back to my school day tomorrow that I have to miss. I don't like being out, because as you may have heard from a friend, or from someone you may have once known who was a teacher, it's a lot more trouble to be away from school than it is to just suck up being sick and go in as usual. My spouse told me to "just pop in a movie for the class; you've got strep throat, for cryin' out loud," which I actually considered for a second before recalling how much my principal and assistant principals wouldn't go for that. They work too hard, and because I see them working hard, I want to work harder, too.

Not to mention my students wouldn't learn as much. And as I explained, I consider myself only a "good enough" teacher.

There's a lot that I could do better. I do have some glorious moments, some crappy moments, and some "Holy mother of pearl, what in God's name am I going to do about this?" moments, but for the most part I'm decent at what I do.

However, there is one thing I am not: a teacher in "receive mode," as you recently put it, who is "waiting to be told what . . . to do." That's what you said about a group of teachers at a school you visited approximately *one* time. One as in once. What the heck?

With all due respect—and I don't mean to raise my voice, so picture me saying this in a very calm yet direct way—do you *know*, do you *fathom*, do you have any *clue* about any or all of the dozens of mini-choices that went into the school day that I'm not even going to *be* there for tomorrow?

Now, let me tell you about my binder. I have an organized "substitute binder" on my desk. To clarify, it's there for a substitute teacher to use when I have to be out. It has tabs. That are labeled. Mmm- hmmm. And sheet protectors. I love that binder. But I wasn't there last Friday, so it may have gotten accidentally moved. And I'm worried about that, Mrs. DeVos. So I need to upload all that crap electronically so that people know what's going on tomorrow and my students don't wander in like a bunch of lost ducklings. Because they're already freshmen, and that's hard enough. That binder has the seating charts, the rosters, the attendance list, the overall plan, the specific daily plan broken down by the hour, a map of the school, the phone number for the school nurse, the number for the school receptionist, the number for the school media specialist, the names of helpful teachers across the hall and next door, the names of helpful students in each class, the emergency procedures, should there be any, of any variety, including a tornado and a fire; plus a couple of paragraphs delineating the difference between a "hard lockdown" and a "soft lockdown" and what to do in each situation. (Although neither of those mentions what to do in the case of a grizzly bear wandering in, although I guess that might call for a hard lockdown, since our school, despite being filled with students who are avid hunters, still think guns in schools would be both frightening and unnecessary and would most likely not be armed at that precise moment, but that's just my gut feeling.)

So, this substitute binder? I was actually, at some point along the line in my teaching, very much told to do it, to put this information together in one place so that anybody walking into my classroom could have all of this important information organized and know what to do. It actually makes good common sense. It wasn't a meaningless mandate, and I wasn't a robot mindlessly executing orders. It essentially covers all the bases, as well as my own rear end. If my teacher friends were reading this they would be thinking, *You forgot lunch duty assignment, hallway monitoring, bathroom passes, and* . . . Anyway.

Ms. DeVos, please stay with me. I know what you are thinking. Why am I telling you all this? Well, it's for the following reason: I haven't included all of that information for my substitute tomorrow because I'm in a "receive mode" and "waiting to be told what to do." I have included it because years of experience and bad substitute experiences have taught me that if I *don't*, the school day in my classroom without me in it won't go very well!

Experience is so very critical in education. Those mistakes we learn from? They make us better.

When we, as teachers, already worry that you are supposed to be leading us as our nation's secretary of education but you have no experience teaching or working in any realm of public education, then you come in and criticize us for a job that requires more details and multitudes of choices than you will ever understand? Ahh! Can you see how that could be mildly flabbergasting and exasperating to us?

Ahem.

Let's get to the fun part: lesson plans.

Those are things teachers write up so that they and their students have a game plan of what to accomplish that day. They include things called "learning goals" and "essential questions," and then you have terms that you might be more familiar with like "date," "agenda," and "homework." Anyway, I was in a bit of a quandary because last Friday my students had finished chapter 14 of *To Kill a Mockingbird*. As you probably know, the dude I referenced earlier in this book, Atticus Finch, has kind of a big part in that story. Anyway, I was planning to be there tomorrow because chapter 15 is my favorite chapter of Harper Lee's book. I have it almost down to a science. I typically lead my students through a discussion on the mob mentality and use snazzy images on my Smart Board to grab their interest and appeal to my visual learners. Then we discuss fascinating topics like "Did you know that kids who are dressed in unrecognizable costumes commit more crimes on Halloween?" and "Did you know that when soccer players see stands filled with fans, they play better? Why do you think that is?" And we talk all about being part of a group and how that's important, but how sometimes you want to break away, but it's too risky and how all the risks that are involved don't always outweigh the benefits of belonging to the group and how hard that can be. And how you shouldn't use run-on sentences.

Then we read the poem "First they came for the Socialists" and talk about what that means, and if you have not read that, Ms. DeVos, you definitely should, and then we actually read the real chapter 15 itself, and I read the beginning of it aloud for my auditory learners, and I put my hand on my hip and walk around the room and talk like Atticus Finch and Heck Tate for entertainment and for effect and to ensure

their rear ends don't dare even *think* about falling asleep at a moment like this. And I'm asking higher-order questions the whole time, and they're raising their hands, and we're debating and discussing; they're giving me great answers, and we're into this thing! And then when we get to the jailhouse scene, I pause for emphasis at the part when the car doors *slam, slam, slam,* and then, then, *then.*
I have them *act it out.* Oh, yeah. It's good. The kinesthetic learners are who I'm trying to appeal to here. They can't help but be at least somewhat into it. The ones who are looking at their friends like they're too cool to do it are the ones I call on.

So they've acted it out, and just at the part when Scout says, "Hey, Mr. Cunningham," I have them all sit down. And they're like, *Okay, lady, let's see where you're going to take this.* And I have my perfectly timed DVD set to those car doors slamming, and the mob from Old Sarum is comin' out, one by one—those good old boys, those good old lovable boys who hold the door open for you and smile at you on the street, but unfortunately only if you're white, and, see, that's just not okay; even if we are on the receiving end of that privilege, so many others are not, and that's not right, and we gotta teach our kids these crucial truths, Mrs. DeVos, don't you agree? We have to keep teaching them, every single day, if we can. We have to find a *way* to teach them, because oftentimes it's not in our standard course of study. Anyway, these men from Old Sarum want to come do something terrible—something heinous—and they are only doing wrong because it's too risky to do right and they don't want to know how to be any different because it's Depression-era Alabama and different is dangerous and nothing makes sense anymore and everybody's so dang hungry all the time. So they're set on doing this thing, on abducting Tom Robinson from the jail cell and lynching him. But then we get to the part where Jem kicks one of 'em, and Scout kicks, and Dill stoically observes Atticus, and then Scout stops it all when she says, "Hey, Mr. Cunningham. I said, 'Hey,' Mr. Cunningham...I go to school with your boy; I go to school with Walter."

And then I won't tell you what happens next, because I have to look out the window because why do I have to cry *every single time at that scene?* But I do. It's just the way she says it. As if Walter Senior didn't know. As if she needed to clarify. It's her innocence. And it's the fact that we're all watching this scene together, and my students are all riveted. Because it's that at least one decent father's life was on the line here, and it was saved by a child, a *child, a child!* And that this crap is happening today. Black lives still don't matter today, Mrs. DeVos, and it's our patriotic duty to make those lives matter, because those lives are sitting at their desks right under our eyes, and yet we're still missing them. We're still not getting it. We're not considering another's point of view even though Atticus told us to.

And we then talk a bit about the Children's March in Birmingham, of which I have a bit of knowledge because I took the initiative (nobody told me to do this) to order an amazing resource from an organization called Teaching Tolerance. They offer resources for free. We teachers do that. We network; we connect; we investigate; we beg, steal, and borrow. We sure as heck don't sit around being told what to do (in case I haven't made that clear yet).

With the Children's March (which you should look up if you don't know about it) we talk about how the bravery of kids *their age* during the civil rights movement ties in with the context in which Harper Lee wrote the novel in the first place. And I turn to my students and say, "*You* are just so-called children. What can *you* do? What can you take a stand for? How do you make *your* voice heard, in small ways, or in big ways?" And I know darn well all of them have different doggone political viewpoints and different religious viewpoints and I must value them all the same. Some will go one way with that question and others will go another way, and it's all good. "Our Class Fits Together" is what my sign says above the board, and I point to it regularly. (I bought that sign with my own money, by the way, Mrs. DeVos. Nobody told me to do it.) No matter what each individual student is thinking when I ask them that question, I relish the wondering, contemplating looks on their precious faces. I get to do that every day. It's a freaking privilege. It's such an unimaginable joy. It's priceless.

But I won't be at school tomorrow for that. So there's no way they can read chapter 15 without me. It's a completely selfish choice, admittedly. I simply don't want to miss the magic.

So I have to think of another game plan. I have to come up with something fun. I create review questions that challenge them to relate each chapter of the book to their modern life and their identity. I edit each question and include clear, specific directions that sound firm but not too mean, like, "You may collaborate with a partner on this assignment. Collaborate means to go through each question together and talk about how to answer it. Do *not* simply split the work in half and delegate questions to each other. It is due by the end of class, whether you are finished or not. Use complete, correctly punctuated and capitalized sentences. Ask each other for opinions and ideas; work together! Proofread your work!"

Then I have to translate a copy of the assignment. At first I accidentally translate it into French because I'm so tired and sick, but then I catch my mistake and translate it into the Spanish that's necessary because I have two students who don't speak English, and I don't tell them to "suck it up and learn the language since they chose to live here." Because I don't know that they *did* choose that. Because when I lived in France for four months, nobody told me to suck it up and learn the language. In fact, many French people wanted to practice their English with me. I was usually treated with privilege and respect. Why shouldn't my students be? I do what I can to help those students, because that's my job. And because I see amazing co- teachers care enough to do it, and I go the extra mile because they seem to be going the extra mile. We keep each other going; we push each other to be better. We don't—you guessed it! —wait to be told what to do.

I won't talk about the papers I have to grade. I got a few done this weekend, but I still have forty-seven short stories to edit, dproofread, and provide meaningful feedback on. No one told me to do this. Nobody told me to assign or grade these papers; nobody will even know if I don't, at least not in the short term. But I genuinely *want* to see what my students can do—not just because I hope they do okay on the End-of-Course exam, which ultimately impacts only their psyche and their self-worth and the public's perception of our school, and how people like you, with all of your money and power and privilege and distance from real people, immediately prejudge the quality of the education of an individual based on a number.

But I'm losing sight of my manners. Please forgive my indiscretion. My internal Julia Sugarbaker sometimes gets loose.

As the matter stands, Mrs. DeVos, I couldn't give three pencil erasers about the numbers. I care about whether or not these youngsters, who will be young adults in the real world so very soon, can use a comma and semicolon correctly and punctuate dialogue correctly and include specific details and imagery and organize their ideas into coherent paragraphs and use the strongest possible word choice, and not end sentences with a preposition although that's really hard to avoid and a million other things I have to teach them, too, but that's just in the one assignment I gave them. I care about whether they can use words as magical tools of power they cannot yet fathom. Power that nobody told me to give them. I just wanted to. I just had to.

Well, this took a little longer than I expected. But as I said, I just wanted you to step inside my skin for a minute and understand my point of view. I wish you the best. But I won't lie, I wish all the public teachers in this country better than the best. And nobody told me to do that.

Kind regards,

Meredith Newlin
Proud Public Teacher

ACKNOWLEDGMENTS

This book has been more than ten years in the making. When I first set out to write it in 2007, the world was significantly more different than it is now. I try to make some sense of all the *poverty* that seems to have taken charge of the world: poverty of conscience, poverty of kindness and compassion, poverty of acknowledging tough truths and doing something about them. The only way I feel any power over the insanity is to remember how the favorite teacher I never had, Mr. Keating from *Dead Poets Society*, put it: one day we'll all be "fertilizing daffodils." So we must remember to seize the day.

There is still so much goodness in the world, and I see deep goodness weaving, wandering, and working through classrooms in the work of dedicated teachers every single day. What we do matters, and what we do is deeply rewarding. Teaching is a worthy, fulfilling occupation. At the time of this writing, I am about to turn 40 years old and am not getting younger; I want to get my message out into the world before the day comes that I am, as Mr. Keating said, "food for worms, lads." We never know when that day will come.

I would like to thank all of the many teachers and educational leaders from whom I have learned and with whom I have worked, who show the meaning of "seize the day" every day in their tireless persistence toward the greater good of their students and society. Through their time, expertise, detailed knowledge of their subject, and irrepressible dedication to their students and their profession, they have inspired and encouraged me beyond measure.

To my class of 21 sophomores, a.k.a. "The Dream Team": Aixa, Bruce, Mark, Chenoa, Karina, Makayla, Amir, Amanda, Carmen, Citlaly, Jaden, Elsa, Dillon, Jyquel, Adanely, Ja'nia, Jennifer, Gorge, Mirta, Magda, Citlali—when I saw your names on the roster last August, I got tears in my eyes because, having taught many of you in your freshman year, I knew I'd been given a special blessing: the gift of teaching you. Thank you for listening to excerpts from this book and offering your support and feedback. Thank you for helping me with the difficult choice of selecting the cover design. Thank you for bringing your very best to class today and helping me love this job. I see and appreciate the real you, and I hope you know it. You truly are the dream team.

Some names in the book have been changed to protect privacy, but special thanks to those former students and teachers who gave permission to use their real names in this book.

I extend deepest gratitude to my hard- working, dedicated parents, Larry and Lee Newlin, for their unwavering, persistent love and belief that I could and would be a writer and a winner, someday. Thank you to my amazing sister, Kathryn Newlin Brown, for reading the book and offering helpful feedback. Thank you to my sister-in- law, Krista Guerrero Argiolas, for listening with rapt and supportive attention to the first chapter, despite the various distractions of family members and little ones running around the living room on a midsummer night. Thank you to my mother-in-law, Tietjen Durham Culp for your love and for being one of the first, if not the very first, to buy this book. Thank you to my grandparents, all my aunts, uncles, cousins, in-laws, and every member of my extended family for their unconditional love and support in so many ways, especially to my great aunt, Dr. Gloria Phillips Turlington, for her wise teaching advice and much appreciated donations of supplies. To my dear friends, mentors, and wider members of my community, thank you for patiently listening to my teaching anecdotes and for helping to uphold the respect that this profession deserves. Mary Sue Olcott and Stephanie Jenal, some potential wrong turns in my teaching path were avoided because you listened, cared, and offered wise ways to get back on track.

Deep gratitude goes to my former student turned professional artist, Jessica Perkins Moncla, for the cover design, and to my former third-grade teacher turned professional editor, Jill Ripley Hughes, for the meticulous copyediting of the text. Thank you to acclaimed author and teacher Zelda Lockhart for always pushing me to pull the truth from the depths and just tell it. Anne Beatty, I have always been in awe of your teaching and writing; I am deeply grateful for your meaningful, helpful feedback and suggestions, but best of all, for our lifelong friendship.

To my brilliant, hilarious, amazing spouse, Catherine, I know you try to keep your hopeless idealism a secret, but the truth is that yours far surpasses mine, and it challenges and makes me better every day. Your unfailing faith, patience, feedback, and support during this process were the final pushes I needed to bring this book to life. Thank you for holding down the fort of our little family when I was spending many a late evening working on the book. I know how lucky I am. You truly are my better half.

To my daughter and son, Eleanor Lucile and Oscar Kemp, my "bright shining one" and "divine champion": you are my world, my dream, and my most magical inspiration for teaching and living.

Being the most and best I can be for you gives me the courage, as Thoreau put it, to go confidently in the direction of my dreams and live the life I've imagined.

And since we're on the topic of being a parent, I would also like to thank the wonderful parents of children I have taught, especially Jennifer Johnson. She and her husband Blake have raised three *incredible* young adults, two of whom I had the honor of teaching, and she has since become a dear friend. My former colleague and mentor, Lori Bartlett Koenig, once said, "I never fully understood my job as a teacher until I became a parent. When I held my first child in my arms, it made me look at teaching completely differently. It was like a lightbulb went off. When my students walk through my door, I know that each one of them is *somebody's baby*." I have enjoyed the good fortune to teach many students whose parents are raising their "babies" with humility, integrity, and a strong sense of social justice. To such parents, thank you for making my work such a delight. I hope I have helped provide just a bit more wind in your child's sails.

To the hundreds (how can that be?) of students who have walked through the doors of my class and lit the room up like fireflies, thank you for so very many things, including your earnestness and faith, and the countless ways you've always made me smile, laugh, and, yes, some days, cry, but above all, thank you from the bottom of my heart for all *you* have taught *me*. Without you, this book would and could never have been written.

Lastly, I give thanks and dedicate this book to you, fantastically courageous teacher. This book is everything I want you, and Jennifer, and Emily, and all new or aspiring teachers to know before they embark on one of the most meaningful and important journeys life has to offer. May they and all of us teachers inspire, as Steinbeck put it, book-waving discussions and new attitudes.

SUGGESTED READING

Bullard, Sara. *Teaching Tolerance: Raising Open- Minded, Empathetic Children.* New York, New York: Doubleday, 1996.

Burke, Jim. The English Teacher's Companion: A Completely New Guide to Classroom, Curriculum, and the Profession. 4th ed. Portsmouth, NH: Heinemann., 2013.

Freire, Paulo. *Pedagogy of Hope.* London, New York: Bloombury, 1992.

Gilbert, Elizabeth. *Big Magic: Creative Living beyond Fear.* New York: Riverhead Books, 2015.

Jackson, Robyn R. *You Can Do This: Hope and Help For New Teachers.* San Francisco: Jossey-Bass, 2014.

Johnson, LouAnne. *Teaching Outside the Box: How to Grab Your Students by Their Brains.* 3rd ed. San Francisco: Jossey-Bass, 2016.

McCourt, Frank. *Teacher Man: A Memoir.* New York: Scribner, 2005.

Nouwen, Henri J. M. *The Inner Voice of Love: A Journey through Anguish to Freedom*. New York: Doubleday, 1996.

Palmer, Parker J. *The Courage to Teach: Exploring the Inner Landscape of a Teacher's Life*. Hoboken, NJ: Jossey-Bass, 2017.

Rademacher, Tom. *It Won't Be Easy: An Exceedingly Honest (And Slightly Unprofessional) Love Letter To Teaching*. University of Minnesota Press, 2017.

Shriver, Maria. *Ten Things I Wish I'd Known . . . Before I Went Out into the Real World*. New York: Warner Books, 2000.

Thompson, Gail L. *Through Ebony Eyes: What Teachers Need to Know But Are Afraid to Ask About African American Students*. San Francisco: Jossey-Bass, 2004.

Whitaker, Todd, Whitaker, Madeline, and Whitaker, Katherine. *Your First Year: How To Survive And Thrive As a New Teacher*. New York: Routledge, 2013.

ABOUT THE AUTHOR

Meredith Newlin has been teaching in North Carolina public schools for 14 years. She has also taught at Rockingham Community College and Duke University Young Writers Camp. She is a graduate of LaVenson Press Studios' Women's Writing Intensive and Full-Length Manuscript Workshop. Her writing has been featured in *Firefly Ridge* Literary Magazine and *NC Boating Lifestyle* Magazine, as well as several custom publications, including in-flight airline magazines such as United Airlines *Hemispheres* and Entertainment Preview; Delta *Sky*, AT&T Wireless Recognitions website; Carlson Hospitality *Voyageur*, and American Cancer Society *Triumph* magazine. She is a native of North Carolina and holds a Bachelor of Arts from UNC-Asheville. She lives in Durham, North Carolina with her family.

Made in the USA
Lexington, KY
10 December 2018